HIDDEN HISTORY
of
MUSIC ROW

HIDDEN HISTORY
of
MUSIC ROW

BRIAN ALLISON, ELIZABETH ELKINS AND VANESSA OLIVAREZ
Foreword by Kix Brooks of Brooks & Dunn

THE
History
PRESS

Published by The History Press
Charleston, SC
www.historypress.com

First published 2020

Manufactured in the United States

ISBN 9781467144568

Library of Congress Control Number: 2020938432

Notice: The information in this book is true and complete to the best of our knowledge. It is offered without guarantee on the part of the authors or The History Press. The authors and The History Press disclaim all liability in connection with the use of this book.

Contents

FOREWORD

When I got to Nashville in 1980, I really didn't know what to expect, but most dreamers like me who wander into town to get into the music business imagine tall high-rises full of executives smoking big cigars, ready to make you a star and cheat you out of your money.

My songs weren't very good then, even though my friends and family had told me they were. But driving up and down 16th and 17th Avenues playing my music for some of the great "ears" in the music business was an education that a writer could get literally nowhere else on the planet. I found out there were no high-rises. Instead, there were these little houses like my grandmother used to live in, except the walls were covered in gold records and pictures of the heroes I had grown up with—and you could hear guitars and pianos up and down the halls trying to find that special melody to go with the rhyme. And there were the studios where the songs that changed my life had been recorded—they were all right there!

I loved that it was small and unpretentious. Folks were nice enough, but you had to have cred to get to "play" inside. That was all I wanted. I worked hard and my songs got better. Eventually, 1212 16th Avenue became my home, and legendary producer Don Gant introduced me to a world that songwriters can only hope they will experience if they die and go to heaven.

It doesn't take five minutes to drive down 16th and up 17th Avenue if you don't stop along the way, but for us, that trip could take all night. You wrote all day in one of those little houses, and then you went on the prowl to see who was around. We would gather at different publishers, where writers like Roger Miller, Mickey Newberry, Rafe Van Hoy and Bruce Channel would sit around and play the songs that were written that day. It was competitive, supportive and inspiring—it was downright magical actually, and it made you want to write the best you had in you so you could play them one of yours! Those two streets have been a true field of dreams, and many big hitters have made history there.

The stories of the characters who wrote the songs and sang them—from Willie Nelson and Kris Kristofferson to Hank Williams and Harlan Howard—live in the walls of those little houses alongside the tales of the promoters and record executives who made people rich and famous. Those stories could go on forever. A music fan could spend his life digging into the tales of 16th and 17th Avenues, and this book is certainly one that does a great job of giving you a unique look into a history that so many of us feel is sacred ground and should not be bulldozed in the name of progress. This fun and fabulous place, this sacred ground of creativity, is called Music Row.

Time marches on, and it will never again be like it was in the '60s or '70s or even the '80s, but it's mostly still here for now. Magic is still being made, fun is still being had and tears are still being shed when all comes together.

The mission and the responsibility still lives up and down those two avenues, like the last words Guy Clark ever said to me before he passed: "Son, go break a heart!"

KIX BROOKS
November 18, 2019
Nashville, Tennessee

Authors' Note

Music Row is as complicated as the musical myths that surround it, both in terms of geography and history. For this book, we define Music Row as the arrowhead-shaped neighborhood stretching from Wedgewood Avenue and Belmont University on the southside, to Broadway and Interstate 40 on the north, with Villa Place as an eastern boundary and Broadway or 18th Avenue as a western one, excluding the intrusion of Vanderbilt University.

It is also important to note that the truth about why and how music is made is often anchored by the memory of those who made it. Stories about its creation—and the places it was made—often change from person to person. We have done our best to hold every source as close to the truth as possible.

Chapter 1

Your Cheatin' Heart

Timothy Demonbreun and the Street that Got His Name

Elizabeth Elkins

Songwriters come to Nashville because they believe in the power of stories in their greatest form: the myth. These song myths are built around the kind of great stories that haunt you—a little bit of the truth, a little bit of a lie and firmly magical. The best country songs arguably create myths of their own: we're all still wondering why Billie Joe jumped off the Tallahatchie Bridge, why a man named his boy Sue and why the lights went out in Georgia that night. Part of Nashville's allure for a songwriter is that one needs to be here—on the streets, in the bars and on the stages—to be a part of its story-making machine. It's a voyeuristic creative life, famously driven by the adage that all you need is three chords and the truth. A few years in, however, and a variation emerges: three chords and a great story.

Locals often remind newcomers that all roads lead down into Nashville. You can come in from the Kentucky hills and cascade south down Interstate 65 past crosswind signs and bourbon makers, dropping hundreds of feet into the city's valley. Or you can come from the west, from the bluffs above the Mississippi, running fast for three hours and slowly descending across the Harpeth River before the skyline juts above the freeway from below. You can speed down Mont Eagle, dodging Civil War ghosts in Murfreesboro before those same skyscrapers stretch before you, their tops only barely visible above the horizon. Or you can drive north through the gentle roll of horse farms in Williamson County and glance at the hill of bones known as Travellers Rest on your right, only to slip further down into land that was once a prehistoric lake bed just as a green sign welcomes you to "Music City Metropolitan Nashville Davidson County: Home of the Grand Ole Opry."

You can crowd around a four-top at the Bluebird Café, eat some barbecue and walk among the former porn shops and pawn shops that now shine like a greener, slower-paced Las Vegas on lower Broadway. You can flip through dusty records at Ernest Tubb Record Shop. You might pull a pillow over your head at the Opryland Hotel at five o'clock in the morning when the ghost of Little Jimmy Dickens begins to sound check "May the Bird of Paradise Fly Up Your Nose" in the atrium below. You can have one heck of a good time among the bachelorette glitz and the rhinestone glamour.

And to get almost anywhere, including Music Row, you'll find yourself on a street with a strange, almost malevolent-sounding name: Demonbreun. It's awkwardly hard to pronounce. Dee-mum-BREE-um? De-mum-BRUM? Demon-spawn? (Insider tip: the locals say "Duh-mum-BREE-um.") It's the name of the highway exit to reach the long avenues of 16th, 17th, 18th and 19th—each block full of record labels and management firms and music publishers, of boys and girls dreaming up gorgeous myths in alleys and Victorian homes in various states of upkeep. Those pickers and grinners, "track guys," lyricists, singers and sign-it-on-the-dotted-line power players? Well, they've only been on the land for sixty-some years. Before that, the man who gave his name to the street that takes a long, slow roll uphill to the Music Row Round-about had a lot going on.

It's rumored that Hank Williams lived right off Demonbreun Street, at the corner of Division Street and 17th Avenue. When he wrote "Your Cheatin' Heart," did he realize that the whole darn city of Nashville began with one heck of a cheating story?

Jacques-Timothe Boucher Sieur de Montbrun (anglicized to Demonbreun soon thereafter), born in 1747 in Quebec, set the bar for country music's stories of cheating, gambling, drinking and being the boss more than two centuries before anybody thought of supporting the storyline with a 1-4-5-4 chord progression and a fiddle.

Lightly called a "fur trader," he came to the city to make his fortune and fame, much like songwriters today. Looking back, it would be easy to call Demonbreun, the son of French Canadian near-royalty and brother to two nuns, a spoiled child who did what he wanted, a classic case misogynist and polygamist, a conceited adventurer. He was a man who conned the Spanish governor out of a war, carried on graceful correspondence with Thomas

The bronze statue of *Musica* sits at the top of Demonbreun Street in 2019. *Elizabeth Elkins.*

A parking deck sits where Hank Williams is rumored to have lived early in his career. *Elizabeth Elkins.*

Jefferson and Alexander Hamilton, owned several slaves, may have served as a spy and was a decorated veteran. He fought in the Revolutionary War— extraordinarily, so it seems, given the number of land grants he received across Kentucky and Tennessee. He's also known around Nashville as the guy who lived in a cave.

His star-like rise and fall, and ultimate arguable redemption (or at least social acceptance), began around 1766 as he journeyed from the province of Quebec to the brand-new Illinois territory, then in French hands. A barely twenty-year-old Demonbreun brought his wife, Therese Archange Gibault, with him, and they eventually settled in the territorial capitol of Kaskaskia, a few paces from the Mississippi River. Their wedding certificate noted that the two were "very much in love." They barely made it to Kaskaskia, however, as a Native American attack en route killed everyone in the party except Timothy and Therese. The two escaped down a river on a quickly assembled raft made of logs and grapevines with only the clothes they were wearing. It was the beginning of a long nightmare at the hands of the native people for Therese.

Once in Kaskaskia, Demonbreun became lieutenant governor of the Illinois territory. The record indicates that he was a reliable, fear-free leader, trusted by many. He was a master of the rivers, running the Mississippi, Ohio and Illinois and eventually heading farther south to the unexplored Cumberland to trap game. Among the looping bends of that river, he found a salt lick frequented by game (this area became known as Sulphur Dell; today it's the site of the Bicentennial Mall) and set up an outpost, taking full advantage of this Shawnee, Chickasaw and Creek Nation hunting, fishing and burial crossroads. He split his time between this new place and Kaskaskia, making the trip several times a year. He swore allegiance to the United States after George Rogers Clark marched into Kaskaskia without a fight. Also on the list of the 128 Frenchmen who pledged themselves to the American cause was a man named Joseph Derrat, a friend who would later play an intriguing role in Demonbreun's life.

In many Nashville history books, Demonbreun is just a footnote, mentioned as an intriguing stranger there before the English arrived, just another of dozens of French fur traders who came and went—notable only as the father of the first white child born in what was then a small trading post known as Fort Nashborough.

But during those years of summers in Kaskaskia and winters trapping along the Cumberland, a curious double life began to emerge. In a cave on the south side of that river, somewhere between Mill Creek and Stone's

River, Demonbreun helped a woman often called his "wife" give birth to his child.

Not many Nashvillians today have seen the cave, but if you stand in the right spot at Shelby Bottoms Park, you can see the entrance above the swirling currents (you can also sneak around Cave Road and Omohundro Road on the south bank, climb down a rotting set of stairs, hang over the side of the rocky bank and shimmy over). It's the only property listed in the National Register of Historic Places in the city that requires a boat trip to see. Demonbreun allegedly used the cave as protection from the natives, using a boat and rope ladder to enter and then pulling the ladder up to prevent access. He also lived there for some time with a woman other than Therese.

And there, in the dark and cool limestone shadows, somewhere around 1784, the Demonbreun myth began.

There is little argument to the fact that Demonbreun had a woman in the cave with him, and they had a baby with blue-gray eyes named William. But wife Therese was back home in Kaskaskia, now battle-scarred after numerous incidents with various natives and raising at least three of Demonbreun's other children. The cave was simply his Nashville home, and the woman, Elizabeth Bennett, was either a mistress or a second wife. Nobody knows Elizabeth's story before she met Demonbreun. Who she is, how she got there, how they met and what those two were really doing in a bat-filled, musty stone room fifteen feet above the racing Cumberland remains unclear. It is unlikely she could read or write, and she left no written trace of her thoughts or motivation. She may have come to the area with an English exploratory party from her birthplace in Virginia; she may have been half Choctaw.

The next fifteen years of Demonbreun's masterful wife-balancing, people-charming and various government-befriending unfold in unclear and dazzlingly weird ways.

The official Demonbreun Society history states that in 1772 Therese "drops out of Kaskaskia records for eight years, accounts say she was captured by Indians." Some early family histories attempt to defend Elizabeth's presence, remarking that Demonbreun surely thought his wife had died at the hands of Native Americans, and he remarried accordingly. However, an examination of his will and an objective view of the children's birthdates leaves no room for defense. In 1788, in fact, he fathered children with both women. Sometime before, he and Elizabeth left the cave behind for a house in the new town, which developed on a ridge north and west of the cave. He acquired several lots.

He and Therese moved to Nashville full-time in 1786. So, for at least six years, Elizabeth and Therese were both in Nashville and both having Demonbreun's children. Elizabeth takes a fall for their actions at least once, showing up in the city's court records in 1787, where she is tried for having a "bastard child." But Demonbreun wasn't satisfied yet.

Researcher William Alexander Provine throws a bigger wrench in things, noting that around this time Demonbreun also lived with a woman by the name of Crutcher, by whom he had no children. Demonbreun also lived with Martha Gray, a woman from Georgia with whom he had a boy and a girl. Provine concluded by stating Demonbreun lived with three women as "common-law wives" in addition to Therese.

BIRTHDATES OF DEMONBREUN'S CHILDREN

By Therese	By Elizabeth	By Martha Gray
1768—Therese Agnes	1784—William	unknown—boy
1770—Felix*	1788—John Baptiste	unknown—girl
1785—Julienne	1792—Polly	
1788—Timothy, Jr.		
1789—Marie-Louise		

*Some sources debate who gave birth to Felix.

So, Hank Williams, step aside—Demonbreun had four wives, likely all aware of one another, and was busy impregnating them as frequently as possible. In the middle of all this love, he managed a tavern, bought more and more land and handled multiple French, Spanish, English—and brand-new American—political influences in middle Tennessee, all the while dealing with constant Native American raids in the still nascent city. In 1791, his two-year-old daughter Mary-Louise was killed in a raid, stolen from Therese's arms and scalped in front of her as the two tried to escape via horseback. Afterward, Therese disappeared from city records, dying either from heartbreak, illness or utter exhaustion. There is no official record of when or where she died; some say that Demonbreun took her all the way back to her family in Boucherville, Canada. Her mother, if still alive, might have reminded her how much she disliked Demonbreun and how hard she fought to prevent the wedding.

Elizabeth, however, had a different destiny. The next year, she made bullets during the raid at Buchanan's Station, fighting alongside Demonbreun and the other white men. The half-French, half-native Joseph Derrat (or

Durratt or Durard or Durrand or Duraque, depending on your source) was also trapped in the raid. The same Derrat who swore allegiance to the United States with Demonbreun in Illinois was now a Native American spy. Something must have changed there, or soon thereafter, as Elizabeth married Derrat in March 1793. These two had children in 1793, 1794 and 1795. There are rumors that some of these offspring were fathered by Demonbreun, and there are local stories that say Demonbreun was asked by city leaders to end his polygamist ways if he wanted to be part of the town, so he married one wife off to his best friend in an attempt to gain more political and social power.

But things get even stranger. Elizabeth and Derrat bought property from Demonbreun, who quickly bought it back. Elizabeth owned Demonbreun's tavern for two years. Derrat spread rumors that the Spanish were preparing to attack the city, which proved false. Elizabeth, Derrat and Demonbreun continued to trade property.

Perhaps it is Elizabeth's story that remains the most interesting. She lived to be at least ninety years old, possibly more than one hundred, operating a tavern (possibly one of ill-repute) north of town known as Granny Rat's. She was kicked out of Mill Creek Baptist Church for immoral behavior. A fighter, landowner, "convicted troublemaker" and mother to at least six children, she's as much at the heart of this myth as the tortured Therese.

Former Tennessee governor William Blount summed up the commonality of those driven to the heart of the state: "Every man who arrives here and determines to become a Citizen appears to feel and I believe does in reality feel an Independence and Consequence to which he was a Stranger in the Atlantic States." These sober and earnest men sang hymns and drank whiskey. They shot natives without regret, held their families close and weren't afraid to throw punches.

But that was never Demonbreun. He predated these careful Englishmen and wild Scotch-Irish. He came with a dutiful sense of Catholicism but a frontier sense of freedom and little need for guilt. He was tough, ambitious and eager to defend his own rights regardless of the ruling countries of the lands, which swayed from native to Spanish to British to French to the United States.

A few stories exist that give us further clues into his personality. There are hints of a temper—stories of the "excitable Frenchman" striking a potential thief across the face at his trading post. In that case, the man was a hunter and Native American fighter who, in response, pulled Demonbreun across the counter and greased him from head to toe in a barrel of buffalo tallow. He fought in a duel in Illinois, killing a man.

There are hints of lawlessness. Court records show that he was fined for retailing liquor without a license at his Summer Street tavern.

There are hints of decorum. In his later years, he never left his home without dressing to the nines in breeches, a ruffled shirt and silver buckles, even after the courtly style had faded. He was hired by the city to keep the streets and courthouse clean. Later in life, he donated land for the first Catholic church in the county.

He was a bizarre mix of rough adventurer and solid citizen, described as "tall, athletic, dark-skinned with a large head, broad shoulders and chest, small legs and a high foot. He wore a blue cotton hunting shirt, leggings of deer hide, a red waistcoat from the French army, and a foxskin cap with the tail hanging down the back." He was part Daniel Boone, part Voltaire.

When the Marquis de Lafayette visited Nashville in 1825, ninety-five-year-old Demonbreun took a seat of honor, and the two spoke happily in French. He received Catholic rites when he died the following October in a house on what is now the corner of Third Avenue and Broadway.

A single paragraph in the *Nashville Banner and Nashville Whig* announced his death: "Died, in this town, on Monday evening last, Capt. Timothy Demumbrane, a venerable citizen of Nashville, and the first white man that ever emigrated to this vicinity."

His will divided his wealth between three legitimate children (Therese Agnes, Julienne and Timothy Jr.) and three illegitimate ones (John Baptiste, Polly and William). Felix was left out. Neither Elizabeth nor the other two women were mentioned.

Even his place of burial remains a contentious argument among descendants from each wife, as the Union army destroyed the city's burial records during the Civil War, turning proof to ash. Demonbreun was most likely buried at a city cemetery near today's First Tennessean Park baseball stadium. Recent newspaper articles indicate that the plot containing his body was never moved, and he still rests in the parking lot behind a Jefferson Street restaurant called Geist. A favorite family story, on the other hand, says that either Elizabeth or John Baptiste exhumed Demonbreun's body from its resting place and reburied him at the family cemetery north of town. The motivation is shady but appears rooted in the concept of true love.

Those clues are not enough to solve the problems that add up to myth that makes his presence so intriguing. Whom did he love? Were they all friends?

Was it all political? Did he assume Nashville would never develop enough and he could always live two separate lives? Did he want Therese for her meekness and Elizabeth for her bravery? How were the Spanish involved in all of this? Was he a spy?

His intentions faded as the city developed around his home and farm. Fort McCook rose on the west side of his property before the Civil War; baseball was played on the grounds after the final shots were fired. Numerous homes and businesses were built along the eponymous new street. By the end of the twentieth century, the east end of Demonbreun was home to the Music City Center and the Schermerhorn Symphony Center. The street's western terminus became a focal point of country music kitsch in the 1970s and 1980s, with businesses like the Conway Twitty Country Store and Record Shop, the Country Music Wax Museum and the Wild West Indian Shop dominating the storefronts. The Country Music Hall of Fame was just steps off the pavement. In 1987, a movement to rename the street "Music Row" due to tourists not being able to pronounce "Demonbreun" was defeated by vocal members of what was obviously a very large group of descendants.

Businesses line Demonbreun Street in 1983. *Nashville Public Library Special Collections*.

Demonbreun Street today still traverses what was once a part of Demonbreun's property, stretching up the hill from the Cumberland River like a several-mile-long arrow shooting west, only to stop cold at the dancing nude statues of *Musica*, each figure clawing for some sort of undefined brass ring, climbing over one another in a race for success, money, power, sex or love. The street's namesake was a cheater, a drinker, a fist-fighter, an adventurer and a European-style Romantic caught up in the dusty spirit of a new frontier. In fact, he was the anti-hero at the heart of thousands of country songs that would later be written on his land.

CHAPTER 2
LADIES ANTEBELLUM

Stories from the Plantations

Brian J. Allison

Well before the first recording studio or music firm ever set eyes on it, the land that would later be home to Music Row already had a long history, full of drama and tragedy, steeped in the American tradition that country music would draw so much of its inspiration from in years to come.

After Demonbreun, a group of Virginians and North Carolinians arrived in the winter of 1779 and the spring of 1780. They built a fort known as the Bluff Station (where downtown Nashville now sits), drew up an instrument of government known as the Cumberland Compact and then got down to their main purpose: dividing up the surrounding land into parcels and establishing farms and plantations.

The first recorded landowner of the area encompassing Music Row was Colonel Elijah Robertson, whose brother James is widely regarded as the founder of the settlement. James and Elijah were Virginians by birth and long served as partners, fighting side by side for the Crown in Lord Dunmore's War and against it during the Revolution. It was for this latter service that Elijah was given two grants of 640 acres each by the Continental Congress. It was an immense tract, stretching from today's Martin Luther King Magnet School on its northern boundary down to Linden Avenue on its south. Upon arrival in the Cumberland settlements, he laid claim to this land, along with many other such claims.

The problem was that this land had already been claimed. The Cherokee, Creek, Shawnee, Delaware, Chickasaw and Choctaw tribes lived in the surrounding area. Bloody fighting between these nations had led to a treaty whereby Middle Tennessee was considered shared ground. People could hunt and trap there and travel through with impunity, but nobody was allowed to settle there; all the nations enforced this policy vigorously. The arrival of the European invaders touched off a bloody fifteen-year war as they fought to defend their territory.

The Robertsons were instrumental in arranging a peace treaty with the powerful Chickasaw leader Piominko, the Prophet Leader, acting on behalf of Minko Homma, the Red King. They met under a large oak tree on James Robertson's plantation, a few miles to the west of Elijah's lands, and signed the instrument of treaty. "The white people…find a good piece of ground…and…go to building houses, which I hope will not be allowed," was the wish of the Red King. In response, the settlers dodged the issue, simply assuring him, "We have buried the hatchet so deep that it is never more to arise." This alliance helped ensure that Nashville would manage to survive when all other hands were turned against them. Forty years later, the Chickasaws' good faith was rewarded with treachery when they were forced to sell their ancestral lands to the U.S. government and move to a new reservation in what is now Oklahoma. It would seem that long before the music industry arrived, broken contracts were already a part of Music Row's story.

Elijah Robertson died on April 14, 1797, of "a sever [sic] attack of the Jandies [sic], on that exses [sic] of drinking sperits [sic]," and the land passed to his daughter, Elizabeth, who was married to Judge John C. Childress Jr., a wealthy and influential jurist. In those days, this property was considerably outside the city limits, and Childress opted to build a country house here in 1813. The result was a spacious brick home, one of the finest and largest in Nashville at the time it was completed. He named it for a poem by Sir Walter Scott, published the same year:

> *That morning sun has three times broke*
> *On Rokeby's glades of elm and oak,*
> *But, rising from their sylvan screen,*
> *Marks no grey turrets' glance between…*

Much like the poet's glades, Rokeby would spread its roots through the entire neighborhood in the years to come.

Oliver Bliss Hayes and his family in 1846. Seated at left is his daughter Adelicia, who became one of Nashville's most legendary citizens and reputedly the wealthiest woman in America by the time she died. *Tennessee State Library and Archives.*

Childress lived here only a short time, but it was said that during those years the guest room was always kept up for General Andrew Jackson, his close friend, who was a frequent guest in the days after returning from his victory in New Orleans. The judge died suddenly in the fall of 1819 at the age of forty-six, and Elizabeth followed in 1822, only forty-three. Five years later, the house was sold to Oliver Bliss Hayes, a fellow attorney and land speculator. It was Hayes's extensive family who would leave their biggest mark on the area.

At the time Hayes purchased Rokeby, the house was the centerpiece of a 250-acre estate that reflected his power and wealth. He threw this fortune into causes dear to him, including education and charitable organizations, among them the Nashville Female Academy, which he helped develop into a prominent school for girls, known across the South. All things considered, it was an appropriate cause for a man who believed that his own daughters should have a first-class education.

There were four sons and four daughters, but it was the Hayes girls who would stand out in public memory. "The three fair maids of Rokeby" would become leading lights in the Nashville social scene of the 1830s and '40s. Beautiful and brilliant, they didn't lack for suitors. Two of them especially would leave a mark on the area around Music Row.

Corinne was the youngest, born on December 19, 1836. In October 1854, when she was eighteen, she accepted the proposal of attorney and planter William Luther Bigelow Lawrence. He recorded the happy occasion in the diary he kept for thirty-four years, writing, "The blind god is triumphant!" On the afternoon of January 24, 1855, Corinne—just turned nineteen— married Lawrence in the parlor at Rokeby. It was a double ceremony, as her sister Laura was married to George W. Shields at the same time. The Lawrences moved into his stately home, Hillside, three quarters of a mile from the house in which she grew up.

But it was elder sister Adelicia who would rise to legendary status, becoming one of Nashville's most storied characters. Born on March 15, 1817, she would earn a reputation for beauty, charm and vivaciousness in her youth. However, this exterior masked an almost ruthless ambition and a brilliant mind far beyond her years. Famously, one day in 1838 she made a social call at Fairvue, the home of Isaac Franklin near Gallatin. He wasn't home that day, but Adelicia apparently had more than just a friendly word in mind. As she took her leave, she reportedly wrote in the guest book with typical boldness, "I like this house, and I set my cap for its master." Good as her word, she married him a year later. The bride was twenty-two and the groom fifty.

Franklin was a tycoon, with a fortune built on misery. One of the largest wholesale slave traders in the South, he had made millions from the buying and selling of human beings. When he died just seven years into their union, it left Adelicia one of the wealthiest and most eligible widows on the continent. She was courted by prominent statesmen and soldiers, and there was wide speculation about whom she would eventually choose. That's why it came as a shock to some of Nashville's society watchers when she married Joseph A.S. Acklen, a relatively unknown attorney from Alabama almost a year younger than herself. It turned out to be a wise choice, as husband and wife made a formidable team investing her money in various enterprises. And it was indeed her money—almost unheard of for the time, the new groom signed a prenuptial agreement granting her control over any money she brought into the marriage. Together the couple controlled land in Tennessee, Louisiana and Texas. The widow Franklin owned acres of cotton and sugar worth millions in today's money, stocks, bonds…and 750 people. She was one of the largest slave owners in Tennessee.

In 1850, the newlyweds built what was meant to be a summer house at the south end of what is now Music Row. Belmont ("beautiful mountain" in Italian) became Adelicia's preferred residence, and by the time the Civil War broke out, it would be her year-round home where she lived a life of unparalleled luxury.

It was, however, the human bondage on which that lifestyle rested that would bring about its end. In April 1861, the nation was torn apart with a cannon shot at Fort Sumter. Nashville fell early on in the struggle, captured in the early spring of 1862. From that point to the end of the war, the city was a fortified camp supporting the Union war effort in Georgia and Mississippi. And the vast acres of the Hayeses, the Lawrences and the Acklens would soon be left gouged by the scars of war.

The army soon built a ring of forts on the southern edge of the city to defend the prize from any counterattack from the south. In 1863, one such fortification was raised on a height just a few hundred yards from Rokeby. Known as Fort Dan McCook in honor of a Union general killed at Kennesaw Mountain in the summer of 1864, it was an ugly, squat earthwork pierced for twenty-six guns. Like the other such fortifications around the city, it would only fire those guns in anger once.

During the Battle of Nashville, the future Music Row was caught between the lines, and all of these symbols of the Old South would suffer for it. Trenches were dug within a few feet of Hillside's front door. At Belmont, Mrs. Acklen would later submit claims for damages done by the troops on her property, assessing the value at a whopping $21,577—more than $300,000 in modern terms. Only Rokeby seemed to weather the storm— and for a surprising reason.

Legend has it that the Hayes family fled the house and left it unlocked for several days during the crisis. They came back after the battle to find nothing amiss, even though several other neighboring houses were ransacked by looting soldiers and citizens. The looters had reportedly given Rokeby a wide berth, all because of the ghost.

The house had long been considered haunted. Family lore maintained that footsteps were heard at night and faces appeared in mirrors. Nobody knew who it was or why it haunted the house, but evidently the marauders didn't wish to face the wrath of the family specter and left the place in peace.

After the war, the trenches were filled in and the fortifications leveled. Fort Dan McCook was completely gone within a generation—the traffic roundabout at the northern end of Music Row marks the spot today. The Old South was gone for good and, with it, the system of slavery that served as its lifeblood. The three plantations fell into a slow and steady decline.

For William Lawrence, it must have been a bitter blow. A lawyer before the war, by the 1870s he was eking out a living as a schoolmaster, his property gradually being auctioned off as he missed payments and taxes. In 1858, he had boasted in his diary that he'd laid in more than 2,500 pounds of pork for the winter, worth nearly $5,000 today. In 1870, he wrote in that same diary, "Killed six hogs of my own raising—the first since Hood's raid, five years ago." Despite the hardships, the couple continued to live at Hillside, the scene of their prewar happiness. Lawrence died in 1902 and his beloved Corinne twelve years afterward, the last of the "three fair maids" to go. Their house went through a succession of owners before being torn down in the early 1950s.

Adelicia was the only one to come out ahead. She flouted the U.S. embargo on cotton sales and sold her crop to the Rothschild family of London for a cool $960,000—all in gold coin. Following the war, her plantation empire in shambles, she sold off most of her remaining property. Chief among these plantations was the one her first husband had named Angola in Louisiana—after the country in Africa where many of the enslaved who worked there were from. This property was eventually sold to Louisiana as the site of the state penitentiary, which is still in operation today. It was here during the 1930s that inmate Huddie Ledbetter would be "discovered" by folk music specialist Alan Lomax. Better known as "Lead Belly," his gritty blues style would go on to influence some of the greatest musicians of the twentieth century, including Johnny Cash. Cash would later record some of his classics at the Columbia Recording Studio on 16th Avenue, ironically making

Rokeby, just days before demolition began in December 1950. The Upper Room Chapel on Grand Avenue now stands on the site. *Nashville Public Library Special Collections.*

Adelicia Acklen the historical bond that brought the two full circle—her family had once owned both the site of the studio and the prison.

Adelicia married a third time and embarked on a series of grand tours of Europe, leaving Nashville in her dust and eventually settling in New York, where she died in 1889. At the time she died, she was reportedly one of the richest women in North America. Her net worth was estimated at more than $8 million. Her beloved Belmont would be purchased and remade into a school for women, later becoming Belmont University, which still operates today at the south end of Music Row.

And Rokeby? The house that started it all? Nothing remains of it today. The decline began when old O.B. Hayes died in 1858. By 1866, the "bottom rail was on top," as the folk saying went among the formerly enslaved. The planters' world had turned upside down so much that part of the former plantation was being used by General William Fisk to house freedmen and women over the objections of Mrs. Hayes. Eventually, Fisk would go on to found the university that still bears his name, one of the greatest African American educational institutions in America. And the school would itself give to the world the Fisk Jubilee Singers, one of Nashville's oldest and proudest musical legacies.

After Sarah died in 1871, the house was acquired by Cornelius Vanderbilt's new university for use as the school's first dormitory. Legend has it the boys staying there while studying divinity and law had several memorable run-ins with the resident ghost at odd hours of the night.

By the turn of the century, the estate had shrunk to five acres, and the surrounding country had been dissected by streets bearing family names: Acklen, Hayes and Adelicia. The old house was run-down and forlorn. A writer named William Sidney Porter visited his daughter, then attending Ward-Belmont College. He visited Rokeby during his stay, and it left an impression. In 1904, writing under his nom de plume, O. Henry, he would immortalize the house as the model for the setting of his story of murder and deceit, *A Municipal Report*:

> *Thirty yards back from the street it stood, outmerged in a splendid grove of trees and untrimmed shrubbery. A row of box bushes overflowed and almost hid the paling fence from sight…when you got inside you saw…*[it was] *a shell, a shadow, a ghost of former grandeur and excellence.…A paint brush had not touched it in twenty years. I could not see why a strong wind should not have bowled it over like a house of cards.*

Eventually, the house became the property of the Methodist Church, and in December 1950, it was ordered demolished to clear the lot for a new, modern building. It went down fighting, and the job took longer than expected due to the solid construction. Even as they destroyed it, the workers admired the "walls three and four bricks thick…broad floors…constructed of cedar planks six inches thick." Some of the wood they pulled out they couldn't even identify. The house was replaced by the Upper Room Chapel, which still occupies the site today at 1908 Grand Avenue. There is no word as to whether the ghost stayed around after being so rudely evicted.

With the passing of Rokeby, the neighborhood finally completed its transition into a rather unremarkable suburban neighborhood. But the earliest residents had left behind a legacy that would be somehow fitting. Lost souls and steel magnolias. The height of luxury and the despair of slavery. Ghostly faces and crumbling mansions. War, loss, patriotism and redemption. And even drinking and a dose of religion.

It would seem that Music Row has long drawn inspiration from the very ground on which it stands.

CHAPTER 3

THE HOUSE THAT FELL DOWN

Vanessa Olivarez

As songwriters, we are always striving for greatness. Reaching for perfection at the golden heart of our craft with every part of our being and throwing it out into the world like stardust, hoping the wind catches even just a fleck of it and turns it into some kind of magic. The let-downs, when they happen (and they do), are tangible. They are a Houdini punch to the gut that leaves the most permanent sort of damage in your willingness to try, as well as in your ego. Every day, we work to write our masterpiece—that one "career song" that everyone wants and no one ever seems to achieve…even when they do. We weave it in our heads for years. The vision of what it means to be successful and what that might look like. I believe to some degree that, in the end, everyone just wants to be appreciated, loved and admired. To have others look upon your opus, the mansion you have built, and think, *This is the result of a grand dream set into motion*. To inspire those people to build their own. Jacob Schnell likely felt the same when he began to build a grand mansion at 1111 16th Avenue South.

Schnell was the son of a German Austrian immigrant family, and his father passed tragically during the ship's Atlantic crossing. In the face of turmoil and hardship, the family used their misfortune as fuel for ambition and were able to procure substantial property holdings in and around Jefferson Street and surrounding areas. They settled in north Nashville, where they opened a general store that in the years to come became a successful feed and seed.

Schnell married lovely young Jennie Powell on September 30, 1873, and the couple had four children together: three girls and a boy. He gave his life to creating a comfortable life for his family. He sought to build a sort of empire where his hard work and years of long hours and drudgery would finally radiate in hues of dark mahogany and gilded Aurelian details. A grand mansion would reflect the honor he had searched for all of his life like a truth-telling mirror. Around the turn of the century, he was able to build the home in a new upper-class development just southwest of downtown. This house was the long-awaited trophy he'd carved himself, and it rose with elegant columns midway down 16th Avenue South. It was a perfect structure he left to crumble, along with the very family he held so dear. Shame, one might say, is a dangerous thing.

Jacob Schnell cursed his home and his daughters to a life of crumbling isolation. *Nashville Public Library Special Collections.*

This house, its trials and tribulations and madness, is much like a songwriter's career. The way Schnell molded nothing into three stories of the finest cut and polished stone, the way he hung the smoothest, roundest Victorian windows the city had ever seen. But he would be sorely disappointed after creating what he thought would be his most prized possession. He made certain that every detail was radiating with intention and thoughtfulness. This lavish and exclusive house was the pinnacle of success for the Schnells. But a dream realized soon became a dream deferred.

"Wooden fluted front columns were sheathed in tin," noted the *Nashville Banner*, examining the once-glorious details in 1974. "The front hall boasted double front parlors, each with a tile-faced fireplace and mantel, and arches with fluted pilasters. The wide stairway similar to other larger Southern plantation houses, was an elongated Y with double flights leading to the second floor, a construction repeated on the third floor leading to the handsome ballroom crown molding and dentil trim embellished the dining room with its bay and five bedrooms were filled with enormous and elaborate tester and half-tester beds, marble topped bureaus and mammoth wardrobes."

But something had gone wrong. Schnell had thrown a party to introduce his three beloved daughters, Betsy, Lena and Bertha; son, Albert, and lovely wife, Jenny, to Nashville's highest society. But it was the dark days of the beginning of the second decade of the twentieth century, the aching years right before the First World War exploded in 1914. Anti-German sentiment was thick across America. No guests came to the party.

The orchestra Schnell hired to entertain his four hundred prestigious invited guests sat silent. Dressed in exquisite formal attire, they waited patiently for the townspeople to come knocking, and to their bewilderment, hardly a soul showed up. The fiasco was doubly humiliating, the wounds permanent. Why didn't the four hundred show up? Well, it's said the "first families" didn't know the Schnells well enough—it was a time when memories of the kaiser didn't sit well with many Nashvillians, and originally they were foreign. His embarrassment grew. It is easy to understand his reasoning for the bleak decision to let the house fall apart. In that moment, he offered a curse to the house: no one shall repair it and no one shall ever leave it. We will let it fall to the ground, an eyesore forever.

It's a moment of "screw it all" that is much like one a songwriter faces when they work hard for everything only to have an entire industry reject or lack interest in their body of work. Working as a songwriter on Nashville's Music Row makes throwing in the towel seem a worthy consideration on most days. Trying, only to be met with the word *no* over and over again, can be quite daunting. To have something you put so much love into ripped apart by words—or silence (which is almost worse), to be treated like the invisible man despite your efforts to be truly seen. We are not instinctively conditioned to thrive at failure's door. The death of a person is not necessarily measured in breaths, but in the number of inadequacies he or she allows themselves to feel. To ingest, like bitter pills we try to spit out, heavy and thick. Like the words on Schnell's tongue when he bellowed out the curse to his family: *Let the house fall down.*

The children listened in rapt befuddlement. And the house began, in the orchestra-muted silence, to fall down around them. When the party was over, and no one showed, Schnell carried out his solemn oath to the community, to the town that had crushed his steel-clad ego. He turned a middle finger back at Nashville and offered a patently southern passive-aggressive action that set the course of his daughters' lives forever. Ironically, he moved from the house the day after the party back to his Jefferson Street store and never came back.

"She said her father had replied that he had built the finest house in the neighborhood and they wouldn't accept him or his family. So he would have his turn. The house would be turned from the finest there to the worst in the region," explained Owen Allen, a realtor and longtime friend of Bertha's. "But he instructed his wife and children they were never to repair one item on the house from that day forward."

The children, in an attempt to obey their father's wishes, stayed as asked for a good number of years. Always honoring the macabre request to never fix a single break of this proverbial glass house, never to fix a burst pipe or a tear in the curtains or a single chipped tile.

Betsy finally married and moved away in the later years, which left Bertha, Lena and Albert (who was rumored to enjoy the "cabaret lifestyle," perhaps coded language for a party lifestyle or a gay lifestyle, depending on who you ask) to live in the old house, which seemed to molt like a poisonous snake. Year after year, it shed its beautiful skin to reveal all of the ugliness of an ache that never leaves you, or perhaps you never leave it. Lena and Albert died in the early 1950s.

It is rumored that Lena remained in the house for at least a week after she breathed her last breath. It's almost as if her promise was so engrained within her that even in death, the ghost of her father would not allow her to leave.

The horrifying condition of the house was described before a late 1974 auction:

> *When the roof began to leak, it was left that way, leaking first to the second floor then to the first where it was caught in rustled containers and buckets. When water pipes froze and burst, the water was cut off, never to be reconnected. A tile bathroom has not been used in generations. Broken window panes were stuffed with newspaper and old cardboard, curtains and shades rotted in place, and fell to the floors.*

Reporters awed and gasped at the unimaginable filth that "Miss Bertha" had been living in. Anything left of value had been stolen by thieves and vagrants, including intricately carved fireplace mantels and banisters. The remaining furniture was sold at auction, bought and sold as if they never mattered. It seems that Bertha never could shake the curse, despite one attempt to sell the house.

"I first met Bertha two years ago when she contacted our office about the listing and selling some of the property including the house," Allen continued. "When we sold one north Nashville piece of property, she had maybe $4,000 in the bank. She listed this house at $100,000 and I had a taker, but she increased the price to $150,000 and he agreed, so she went

The house that fell down. *Metro Nashville Archives.*

to $200,000 and he quit. She never intended to leave it alive. I told her she would have to sell it, and she said it hadn't fallen in yet, she would stay until it did."

In her final years, she rarely cooked. Some days, employees of a Schnell-owned nightclub on Jefferson Street brought her a meal. They would also do her grocery shopping and run her general errands. She would pace almost neurotically like a mink, high on the second story. Passerbys said it looked like the balcony was disintegrating under her feet. Occasionally, she would talk warmly with people walking by. The ones who knew her thought her to be well spoken and highly educated. She hung out often in the dining room, which was converted into a broke-down parlor of sorts, complete with boarded up windows, a small space heater and an old dog named Andy to keep her company. There she'd rest for her final days, reading current events to keep up with the perpetually spinning outside world.

"She nearly always wore rags," Allen remembered. "More in warm weather, less in cold, safely pinned together. Once I took my wife to visit her, and I almost didn't recognize her. She had cleaned up, wore a dress and make-up and had her hair fixed. But the filth was the same. We just stepped over it."

The auction revealed that every room was exactly like the next, full of dirt and muck and sadness—every room but one. When Bertha's mother left the house so many years before, she made a solemn promise to return to her isolated family (though she never did), and so the children kept her room as pristine as the first day they settled in. Her bed, brought over by boat to this country, sat perfectly made, and the furniture was even dusted. It was as if they had expected her arrival at any moment. Nonetheless, everything worth anything in the house was auctioned. Owen Allen, along with dealer and appraiser Agnes DeMoss and a court-appointed executor, directed the sale of the house and the many items inside. It sat empty and unwanted until the spring of 1977, when a wrecking ball crashed Schnell's dreams permanently to the ground.

Many students at Belmont University referred to 1111 16th Avenue South as the Haunted House; even after its demolition and rebirth as Capitol Records, there was always a feeling that the new building was simply a face to hide the spirit of that property, but ghosts cannot be glazed over. The past cannot be erased. I believe that once a person exists, the energy of that person remains in the world, particularly if there is some form of unfinished business. I remember plucking away at electronic keyboards in dark rooms late in the evening at 27 Music Square West, my old publishing house at BMG. I would often hear voices and noises—creaks and cracks and footsteps that sounded like someone trying not to make a sound. Echoes of old visions and songs. I would wonder at the many noises, mostly trying to ignore them out of my own fears. But always listening, listening to the failures and triumphs of so many skilled and poetic songwriters who graced those hallways and writing rooms. Hoping to snag just a word or a melody or a turn of phrase. Chasing the muses of geniuses past. I believe the unfinished business keeps these sacred buildings of Music Row always spirited.

It is reported that after Capitol Records moved into the new structure at 1111 16th, apparitions of the girls still remained. Employees of the famed record company began to notice objects moving on their own, doors being locked from the inside, lights being turned on and off and windows found open that had been closed and locked. People quit working there, telling their supervisors they could not get used to the strange happenings, including eerie "visits from the Schnell daughters." Cold spots were common throughout the building, and phone lines from unoccupied offices would ring all on their own accord. Tapes in the recording studio would fly off the reels unexpectedly or unravel overnight. The building fascinated psychics and ghost hunters alike. Phyllis Moline, a local medium, described the location as a "confusion of emotions." Reporters from the *Tennessean* and WSM-TV claimed that the ghost sisters threatened them. Allegedly, when Nashville

Big Loud Shirt, home of country artists Florida Georgia Line, now occupies the 1111 16th Avenue lot. *Vanessa Olivarez.*

songwriter Craig Wiseman moved his publishing company, Big Loud Shirt, into the building, a medium was brought in to clear it of any remaining visitors, easing the mind of new and nervous employees. Rumors of the sisters, however, are still around.

It's hard to imagine what would have happened if someone had saved the home and restored it to its original grandeur. Would Schnell have been angry that his curse had been denied? Would he storm the halls and shake the columns? Or would he smile, secretly happy that his house had found a home on Music Row, creating songs never played by the orchestra he hired?

The story of the Schnell house sends my mind wandering back to the many days I have pondered quitting music altogether. I have had so many "almosts." Finite triumphs I thought would escalate into illustrious moments in the sun. Bright spots to carry me through the rest of it and make the occasionally miserable climb to the top of hell's mountain seem a little less so. I have written a great many songs—songs that hold an immense amount of weight for me emotionally. I have spent hours on even the most unimportant details. I have waited for the light to shine on me with the ease of a steady afternoon breeze just once, only to discover an avalanche of endless struggle. I remember the way it lifted me to almost sky level to have a single with a major label artist (Billy Currington's 2015 "Drinkin' Town with a Football Problem"). I built the victory in my head to be some sort of debut for me. Everyone believed within their core that this song would be not only a no. 1 but also a multi-week hit song that would make us all a lot of money. But the money wasn't the thing that was driving me; it was the anticipation of finally feeling like someone was listening. The excitement of my family and friends as Venus-bright stars danced in their eyes and blinded them. And me. The stress and nail-biting hours of waiting for the always dreaded "see what happens" in the coming weeks. Watching the chart every morning. Praying for it to climb into the 30s…20s…teens. And the fall of that hope as the song dropped off the charts at no. 29 and seemingly out of people's memories. It all happens in a lightning flash. Heartbreak is a part of life. It makes us humble. Failing gracefully is an immeasurably valuable skill, and with the career I have chosen, I have become a master. Still, I forge ahead steadfastly in the direction in which I began. My compass seems to be stuck; I believe Jacob's just gave out.

CHAPTER 4

THE CLOSER TO CHURCH, THE NEARER TO GOD

Old-Time Religion

Elizabeth Elkins

Around 1900, the avenues that would become Music Row had different names. Along these thoroughfares—known then as Belmont (16th), Addison (17th), Lamar (18th) and Everett (19th)—numerous churches and church-sponsored homes thrived. Cross streets that would later hold the names of music legends like Chet Atkins and Roy Acuff were known as Elizabeth and Catron. The first three decades of the twentieth century were a housing boom for the area, with new homes rising from the avenues most frequently between 1910 and 1930. It quickly became one of the city's most desired new "streetcar suburbs." Churches and religious spaces followed the neighborhood's bustling development. Many of these spaces and the joyous noises found within would later house the seeds of Christian music that spread across the globe. Others have been threatened by the wrecking ball, the ghosts of their triumphs and tragedies cursed to haunt the steel and glass towers of twenty-first-century progress. In a town known as the golden buckle on the Bible Belt, there's truly a church on every corner.

LITTLE SISTERS OF THE POOR HOME FOR THE AGED, 1400 18TH AVENUE SOUTH

Little Sisters of the Poor is a Roman Catholic order that takes care of the elderly poor. Each Home for the Aged is run by nuns who share in everything with the residents, including living in the home and eating the same meals. The order came to Nashville as a part of its early twentieth-century reach across the United States from its headquarters in France. When the group's property on Main Street in East Nashville burned to the ground in the great fire of 1916, the organization chose a two-acre lot at the corner of Horton and 18th Avenues to build an even grander space: four stories of yellow brick and steel. There they crafted a grand Renaissance Revival home, including a sun porch off every room for bedridden patients. The original entrance on Horton boasted massive Tuscan columns, between which one can still read "Home for the Aged" arched across the stone frieze.

When the new home opened in 1917, it could house one hundred patients. Conditions for admission stated that the applicant be "destitute, of good moral character, and 65 years of age with no income. No distinction is made for creed or nationality." However, only whites were allowed admittance until the 1960s. Visitors could only drop by daily from 2:00 p.m. to 3:00 p.m. Sister Jane, who ran the home, entered the work of the order in 1908 at Saint Servan, France. She took her vows on Christmas Day 1900 and then

The Little Sisters of the Poor Home for the Aged, 1400 18th Avenue South. *Elizabeth Elkins.*

traveled to the United States, working in homes in Albany, New York, and Washington, D.C. After returning to France for her final vows, she headed to Chicago, where she received her appointment as mother of the Nashville community. In Nashville, she was well liked, known as one of the happiest women in town and was admired for her "attractive French pronunciation of American words."

There were many interesting employees and residents, perhaps the most interesting of whom was Spanish-American War veteran and convicted murderer Miller Horn. Horn, who grew up in far east Tennessee, headed west to be a cowboy and ended up riding up San Juan Hill with Teddy Roosevelt as a part of the famous Rough Riders. When Horn returned from Cuba, however, things went south—all because of farm animals. In 1912, he received a ten- to twenty-year sentence at the Tennessee State Penitentiary for killing a neighbor over turkeys in 1912. He was freed soon thereafter when evidence indicated that it was self-defense (his story all along). Sixteen years later, however, he was back in court for fatally shooting three members of a tenant farm family over a cow. He had numerous bullet wounds after that argument, and doctors didn't expect him to live more than a few days. A man who had married three times and claimed to have never had a drink—"not even a dose of medicine" his whole life—Horn was given a life sentence in the notorious Brushy Mountain prison in Morgan County, Tennessee, later made famous when Dr. Martin Luther King Jr.'s killer James Earl Ray attempted to escape it. Horn, however, did escape from Brushy Mountain for an afternoon, and after he was caught, he learned that the Supreme Court would hear his appeal. Once again, Horn was freed when evidence indicated he was acting in self-defense. Whether it was a case of friends in high places, or wrongful imprisonment initially, the resulting freedom led to various spots working on farms around Nashville before a priest transferred him to work at the Little Sisters of the Poor. He couldn't stay long though.

"I should have stayed at the 'Little Sisters,'" he told the *Tennessean*. "They were good to me there. Maybe too good. But the place had stone walls around it. The walls weren't for punishment, understand—probably more for protection of the ones inside. But—stone walls—I don't even like to talk about them."

In many cases, the home provided shelter and healthcare for men and women who had nowhere to go. Sometimes, shared poverty brought families in. In December 1955, Home for the Aged residents and sisters Mary and Nellie Corcoran died just a half hour apart. The daughters of a Charlotte Avenue grocer, the two were inseparable and had been living in the building

A side view of the Home for the Aged as renovation began around 1997. *Steve Armistead.*

for six years. No one knew their ages, but the two bodies lay in state together for a requiem high mass in the building's chapel.

An increase in federal welfare and a reduction in the number of Sisters joining the order led to the Home's closing in 1968. Sister Amedee noted that the encroachment of so many college campuses around the home discouraged many elderly from wanting to live there, and the population was low.

From 1968 to 1975, the home stood vacant, a behemoth on the western rise of 18th Avenue, until it was purchased and converted into a series of nursing homes, including the Belmont Health Care Center and Carriage Health Care. It was during this period that things took a somewhat darker turn, from rumors of patients throwing themselves out of the upper windows to their deaths to hints of burnt-out staff eager to leave.

Steve Armistead, co-owner of Armistead Arnold Pollard Real Estate Services, was working at Armistead-Barkley Inc. when he had an idea that likely saved the building. He knew that music industry giant Bertelsmann Music Group (BMG) was looking for a new home on Music Row. He saw

The Home for the Aged chapel prior to renovation. This is where patients sat with "tiny televisions" during its use as a nursing home. The chapel became a setting for no. 1 song parties. *Steve Armistead.*

potential in the decaying Home for the Aged and was the force behind its transformation from a run-down nursing home to a record label's home base showplace.

"We like to take old things and restore them," he said. "The space was in terrible condition; it was really rough, truly an indigent nursing home in disrepair. I knew we had to do a total renovation. The scenes I saw inside unfortunately reminded me of the film *One Flew Over the Cuckoo's Nest*. You walked in, and it smelled just awful. I remember the chapel area very well. People were sitting in there watching tiny televisions. It was clearly in bad shape, people and building, and not being run well. People asked me if I felt bad kicking people out, but I knew the situation was so bad that it was certainly helping people in the end to change it."

By that point, only a small portion of the 100,000 square feet was being utilized, with the top floor completely empty. Armistead was able to meet with the owner (who was offsite in Huntsville, Alabama), making him an offer that was immediately accepted.

A Home for the Aged dormitory building, where pentagrams were allegedly later found etched in the attic floor. *Steve Armistead.*

Armistead recalled workers telling stories of seeing and hearing ghosts throughout the space, especially in a separate dorm area where the nurses live. They opened bricked-up windows and restored original wooden bannisters. Floors once painted military gray were stripped to reveal the original marble. The team found a time capsule behind the stones on the Horton Street side. There nuns had placed statues of Jesus, Mary and Joseph.

In 1999, after eighteen months of work, BMG moved in. The once dilapidated chapel became the center point, hosting many concerts and "Number One Parties" (events held for the artists, writers, radio reps and label professionals when a song reaches no. 1 on the charts). The building itself won a Metropolitan Historical Commission Architectural Award that year and a spot in the National Register of Historic Landmarks.

BMG later sold to Sony, whose building manager recalled kicking out a man living in the "haunted" dormitory building's attic. The man was burning black candles and etching pentagrams on the wood floors. In 2014, Sony sold the Home for the Aged to Vanderbilt University for more than $12 million. Perhaps the Catholic sisters knew that a surrounding college would eventually move in, although they might nod in slight French approval if they learned that nursing students take classes in rooms where people like Mary and Nellie Corcoran died.

THE CHURCH OF THE ADVENT, 1200 17TH AVENUE SOUTH

This Gothic building has no shortage of diabolical secrets—and hit records. The Church of the Advent, an Episcopalian denominational church, laid its cornerstone on the southeastern intersection of 17th Avenue and Edgehill Avenue in December 1910. Its building began with an argument at Christ Church on Broadway, where a dispute over pew rentals led a disgruntled group to start a new church. The offended group chose this property in what was then a burgeoning streetcar suburb to build this graceful stone building for its new congregation.

The passing streetcars would clearly have a strong effect on playwright Tennessee Williams, the grandson of Reverend Walker E. Dakin, an early rector. Williams lived in the rectory annex across the street from 1916 to 1917. That annex has since been torn down. His time in Nashville clearly influenced his future writing; perhaps it planted a seed for his famous play *A Streetcar Named Desire*. "I loved Nashville," he told *Tennessean* writer Louise Davis. "I remember so many things about it—picking flowers…a terrible thunderstorm that tore the awning off our porch…and I had my first streetcar ride in Nashville."

After the Church of the Advent departed for suburban Brentwood in the 1970s, the building changed hands several times, including to the YMCA. But it is most notably the legend of Tony Alamo, a televangelist who used the building in the 1970s and '80s, that haunts its stone walls today. Alamo preached anti-Catholicism, anti-homosexuality and anti-government. His followers gathered weekly to hear him "preach" at the church, although he had outposts across the United States. Followers were expected to give him their possessions, renounce their families and work in his clothing sweat shops (of note: Elvis Presley, Dolly Parton, Conway Twitty, Prince and Madonna are said to have worn his trademark "Tony Alamo of Nashville" sequin-embellished denim jackets). In the meantime, Alamo was funneling millions of tax-free dollars through the church. One of his mantras was "God wants his children to go first class."

When Alamo's wife died, he allegedly kept her in a freezer in the church's basement, occasionally shocking her dead body with electricity to try to bring her back to life. He blamed the congregation when his experiments failed. Today, the freezer houses the reverb plates for the recording studio. Alamo spent time in prison for tax evasion and was later convicted of child abuse following revelations that he had sex multiple times with teen and preteen girls he transported across state lines (and considered to be his "wives").

The Church of the Advent at 1200 17th Avenue South—once known for dead bodies in the basement and Tennessee Williams—is now one of Nashville's most famous recording studios. *Elizabeth Elkins.*

His demise was a fortunate situation for Ocean Way Studios' Allen Sides, who was looking for a Nashville outpost of the famous Los Angeles studio. He and Gary Belz of House of Blues studios purchased the property easily from Alamo and redesigned the interior for a world-class recording space. As of 2019, Ocean Way is one of the most vibrant studios remaining on Music Row. The client list reads like a who's who of contemporary music: from country stalwarts like Tim McGraw, Luke Bryan and Garth Brooks to metal giants Megadeath and back around to pop icons Christina Aguilera and Matchbox Twenty. The century-old church is considered one of the best recording facilities in the United States. Sony Playstation, Electronic Arts video games and Lionsgate films have also used the stained-glass lit space to score projects. It is now owned by Belmont University.

Belmont Church, 68 Music Square East

In 1911, the corner of 16th Avenue and Grand Avenue was the site of a wildly popular two-week tent revival. Just four years later, when the road was still gravel, the brotherhood of the Churches of Christ erected a large and powerful Greek Revival chapel building: the Belmont Avenue Church of Christ.

The Church of Christ is one of the more conservative sects of southern religion. In Nashville, it is anchored by the looming presence of David Lipscomb, founder of the Church of Christ and his eponymous Green Hills academy and university. In addition to a close and literal reading of the Bible text as absolute, the Church of Christ is known for a rule that feels like an oxymoron in Music City: no musical instruments can be used to praise the Lord. In the 1970s, the then-renamed Belmont Church stood on the more radical side of a separation within the church that became known as the "Belmont Movement." Led by many college students, this group relaxed some of the more stringent Lipscombian ideals toward a more forward-thinking, nondenominational church. Musical instruments—and people who believed in a more lenient form of faith—were allowed to join. The church quickly became the central gathering point for Belmont College students who wanted to praise Jesus in a new, more liberal way.

Across Grand Avenue at 1001 16th Avenue South was a former H.G. Hill grocery store. In 1973, the abandoned store had a rustic interior covered with barn wood. There was an old, wood burning stove sitting on top of a worn patchwork carpet. That year, a man named Bob Hughey was asked to run a new ministry for Belmont Church called Koinonia. Designed as a coffeehouse/bookstore to attract the community of "hippies, young people, and street people who frequent the downtown area of Nashville," the coffeehouse area included a place for guitar players. The space soon became one of the most popular hangouts in the area. Worship leaders like Amy Grant and Michael W. Smith wrote songs and discussed Jesus Christ in praise gatherings that became so well attended that the place was considered a fire marshal's nightmare. The Church of Christ elders sent letters, worried that evil had taken over. By that time, there was no stopping the new movement. In this corner coffee shop with no air conditioning, the combination of musicianship and faith would create a brand new non-secular pop genre originally called "Jesus Music," which would become CCM, or Contemporary Christian Music.

Left: The Belmont Avenue Church of Christ angered the Church of Christ when it allowed musical instruments as a part of praise. *Elizabeth Elkins*.

Right: Koinonia, where the Contemporary Christian Music genre began. *Elizabeth Elkins*.

Grant believed that the magic of the space was the collision of culture on Music Row.

"This was not a pristine group of people," she said. "It was ragtag and nobody had it together, but everyone was captivated by this incredible experience of community that came because of this spirit of God."

Koinonia would launch the careers of not only Grant and Smith but also producer/songwriter Brown Bannister, Chris Christian, Annie and Steve Chapman, Bruce Carroll, Michael Card, Rich Mullins, Buddy Greene and the band Dogwood. Dogwood's Steve Chapman explained, "Our lyrics were biblically based, but our melodies bore the mark of the secular music of the times. We had no idea that we were helping pioneer CCM. Koinonia was a gift from heaven. It was a training ground for us."

At the time of publication, the Koinonia property was set to become a luxury hotel.

Addison Avenue Cumberland Presbyterian Church, 114 17ᵀᴴ Avenue South

At the turn of the twentieth century, the Addison Avenue Cumberland Presbyterian Church built a handsome brick sanctuary in this location. To celebrate its construction, the pastor was given a rare silver half-dollar dated 1810, the year of the organization of the Cumberland Presbyterian Church. It was laid in the cornerstone of the church and perhaps is still hidden in the dirt there today. In 1951, the congregation relocated and sold the property. It was a VFW post until Monument Studios moved in in 1968. Numerous stars recorded there including Elvis Presley, Kris Kristofferson, Reba McEntire, the Statler Brothers, Willie Nelson, Delbert McClinton and Johnny Cash. Monument would continue to operate until 1975. Since then, the former church building has been occupied by a number of recording studios, including Studio One, owned by Tommy Strong and Mort Thomasson (1976–77); Young'un Sound Studio, owned by guitarist Chip Young (1977–89); and Masterlink, owned by Al Jolsen Jr. (1990–2010). It is currently the home of Zac Brown's Southern Ground studio.

The Addison Avenue Cumberland Presbyterian Church is now Southern Ground Nashville studio, but this back view shows off more of the original structure. *Elizabeth Elkins*.

Scarritt Bennett, 1027 18ᵀᴴ Avenue South

The Wightman Chapel at the Scarritt Bennett Center was a part of the Scarritt College for Christian Workers, then a part of the Methodist Church. Built in 1928, it is named after Maria Davies Wightman, president of the Women's Board of Foreign Missions of the Methodist Episcopal Church from 1894 to 1908. A pioneer in women's rights, she advocated for the training of women as missionaries for the denomination. Built in classic Gothic style, the chapel also played a role in the civil rights movement when Reverend Dr. Martin Luther King Jr. preached there on April 25, 1957. The topic? "The Role of the Church in Facing the Nation's Chief Moral Dilemma."

The Upper Room, 1908 Grand Avenue

The Upper Room, a Christian printing company known for its daily devotionals, began publishing in 1935. The company's Nashville headquarters, which includes a chapel, was constructed on the site of Judge Oliver Bliss Hayes's antebellum home Rokeby. Hayes was the primary owner of the majority of the land that would become Music Row. The chapel features an 1853 wood carving of *The Last Supper*, based on Leonardo da Vinci's famous painting, by Italian sculptor Ernest Pellegrini, plus an eight-by-twenty-foot stained-glass window. The museum contains religious artifacts and paintings.

Although the twists and turns of the music industry continue to underscore the intent of the original adage "the nearer to church, the farther to God," these spaces are a reminder of how country music so often walks the line between hymns and secular pop. Although no church on Music Row looms as large in Nashville's music history as the original "Mother Church," the Ryman Auditorium, each is a unique part of the mystery and sound that made Nashville famous. From the rock-and-roll at Ocean Way to the pop hymns at Belmont Church, each is a reminder of the faith and outreach of those who once lived in the neighborhood and the old-time religion at the heart of much of country music.

CHAPTER 5

IT ALL BEGINS WITH A SOUND

Brian J. Allison

T he rise of Music Row in the early 1960s was swift and spectacular. It coincided with the coming of age of country as its own art form, when it developed from its rather simple roots into something unique. In a remarkably short time, Nashville became the heart of the recording industry for this new genre. It would prove to be a golden age— the age of the "Nashville Sound."

The city has a long musical tradition, but it didn't become identified for it until the middle of the twentieth century. For example, the city has been home to the internationally famous Fisk Jubilee Singers since 1871. The historically African American college was founded after the Civil War to educate the newly freed and their children, and the Singers toured to raise revenue for the institute. Eventually, the group's spellbinding talent took them on international tours, and in 1873, they performed before Queen Victoria herself. The monarch is said to have replied that Nashville must be a "city of music." And thus the city earned the nickname "Music City."

Or so a recently popular story goes. It seems the locals love a good story, but sometimes they don't let facts get in the way. While the Jubilee Singers are one of the proudest musical traditions to call the city home, unfortunately there seems to be no basis to the story. No documentation exists that Nashville was ever called by that nickname until the year 1950. In fact, it was the country music industry that coined the nickname when David Cobb, announcer for Red Foley's radio program, memorably told the audience that the show was coming to them from "Music City, U.S.A." The name stuck, and Nashville—once known as the "Rock City"—acquired a new and much more memorable moniker.

Nobody really knows how Music Row acquired its title, but it isn't hard to guess. In fact, the name isn't even unique. During the 1940s, 48th Street in New York City was also called "Music Row" due to the number of record and music stores lining the street, so it's likely the name was simply borrowed. If so, it's fitting. Nashville's version would not only eclipse the fame of the original but would also come to dominate the industry itself.

During the 1940s, New York and Los Angeles were the centers of audio recording in the United States, and most of the major record labels such as RCA, Capitol, Liberty or Decca were headquartered in one or the other. It should also be noted that there really wasn't any such thing as "country music." Instead, it was generically—and rather insultingly—referred to as "hillbilly music," a mishmash of old mountain ballads, cowboy songs, bluegrass and other traditional styles. But times were changing.

Nashville became associated in the public mind with the premiere of the *Grand Ole Opry* in 1926 on WSM radio, and gradually more and more artists began to call the town home in the next few decades. By the mid-1940s, there was a budding recording industry, and several small studios were established in different locations across town and in the suburbs. Still, there was little incentive for outside artists to come to Nashville when other cities offered more advanced facilities.

The birth of Music Row can be traced to the early 1950s and two brothers named Bradley. Owen and Harold Bradley were born in nearby Sumner County but came to Nashville as youngsters, where they grew up playing music in local venues. Harold would become one of the most legendary studio musicians in town, while Owen moved from performing into songwriting, arranging and production.

By 1954, he and Harold were operating a studio in Hillsboro Village on 21st Avenue South, but they were dissatisfied with the acoustics at that location. At the time, Owen was working as an arranger for Paul Cohen of Decca Records of New York. Cohen usually worked in two-week marathon sessions, flying into Nashville and out once more, but he found working in the city frustrating due to the lack of a state-of-the-art studio. Cohen was thinking of moving his operation to Texas when Bradley asked him, "What if we built a studio here?" Cohen agreed and pledged his support, saying he intended to schedule at least one hundred sessions for Decca at the facility to get the project off the ground.

With that in mind, Harold and Owen purchased a small house at 806 16th Avenue South that had recently been rezoned as a commercial district. They were attracted by the low price of real estate in the neighborhood, and the brothers put down $7,500 for the property. The house was gutted, and the basement was converted into the studio they wanted. For the same amount of money, they purchased an army surplus Quonset hut. Working from a prefab kit, they installed it in the back yard, intending to use it as a television studio. However, the audio side of things quickly outgrew the house and moved into the little steel structure, and it was as "the Quonset hut" that the operation became known.

Bradley's studio eventually paid for itself many times over, and its reputation became legendary. It marked the birth of what would become Music Row.

The sound quality from the Decca sessions turned heads, and other labels such as Capitol and Columbia began booking sessions there. Then others began moving into the neighborhood. RCA was first off the bat, opening Studio B and an office on 16th Avenue in 1957, and many other major labels began to gravitate to the area. By 1961, Cedarwood Publishing and the Atlas booking agency had joined them. And it was around this time that the area acquired its nickname, with local papers advertising "Music Row…Exceptional Locations…Competitive Prices." The boom was on, and the Bradley brothers' gamble paid off handsomely. In 1962, Columbia Records bought them out for $300,000—a rather tidy return on their original investment.

According to a story told by Owen's son Jerry Bradley, the Columbia executives who came to Nashville to finalize the sale were still scratching their heads about how the studio's distinctive sound was achieved. They questioned him about the tarpaulin stretched across the top of the structure, which Owen had placed there to dampen the reverb off the floor and the steel walls. Later, after signing the contract, Bradley found the two suits on a ladder, apparently looking for the hidden secret device under the tarp. "Hey," one of them said in surprise, "there ain't nothin' but curtains up here." He just smiled and replied, "I told you!"

They had a right to be surprised. Many of the "secrets" of Music Row were simply the results of talent, hard work and a good deal of monkeying around. The technology was brand new, with magnetic tape only having come on the market since the end of the war, so much had to be improvised or discovered through trial and error.

For example, Owen added what his brother referred to as "shed houses"— in other words isolation booths—and baffles between musicians used to

Willie Nelson, photographed during a session for his first album in 1961 at Owen Bradley's Quonset Hut studio on 16th Avenue. The legendary Anita Kerr singers are backing him up. *Left to right*: Gil Wright, Anita, Willie, Dottie Dillard and Louis Nunley. *Joe Allison Collection*.

isolate sound for stereo recordings. The musicians were often hired in the morning for a session that same afternoon rather than weeks or months in advance, as is the case nowadays.

Sometimes there were unique problems to overcome. In 1961, when Willie Nelson recorded his first album in Nashville, producer Joe Allison recalled that nobody wanted to cut him. As Hank Cochran put it, "They think he sings funny." His phrasing was incredibly sophisticated and so unique that the other musicians in the studio were often thrown off by it. Allison talked it over with Harold Bradley. Harold was a master, and he had the reputation of being able to keep up with artists as diverse as Bill Monroe and Sinatra, but even he said, "I don't know...I've never heard anything quite like him." The two took a drive to discuss how to pull it off. Bradley finally told him the best thing would be to sit back, "play rhythm...and don't get in the way." It worked.

And it worked because of the raw talent available, and not just out front. Often mentioned but rarely praised, Nashville was home to some of the finest session musicians in the country. The Anita Kerr Singers and the Jordanaires—along with an army of hungry, talented guitarists, bassists, pianists and drummers—ensured that this developing genre would have a crisp, unique flavor. By 1957, a new phrase had been coined to describe it: "the Nashville Sound."

It marked a transition in musical style that was just as radical as the development of rock-and-roll. "Hillbilly music" was evolving into country, with elements borrowed from popular music, like rhythm sections and backup singers, and which eschewed traditional instruments such as banjos and fiddles. In a world where country continues to evolve and embrace such cultural elements as hip-hop and hard rock, it might surprise many today to realize that such departures are not new; they were also just as controversial then. Famously, the *Grand Ole Opry* had a long-standing ban on electric guitars and drums. And while the *Louisiana Hayride* grudgingly accepted them, the drummer reportedly had to play from behind a curtain so the audience couldn't see him.

The new sound revolutionized the industry, and singers had hits that were often able to cross over into the mainstream pop charts, as Skeeter Davis would with "End of the World" in 1962 and Roger Miller with "King of the Road" three years later. Ironically, while the rise of rock-and-roll is often regarded today as a revolution in musical style, a quick survey will show that in the late '50s and early '60s, it remained in its infancy, a "novelty" style aimed at a juvenile market. Country, which was developing right alongside it, turned into something far more refined. There's more than a little truth in the trope that country songs are always about lost love and drinking—from the outset they were dealing with more "mature" themes.

By the early 1960s, Music Row was growing hand over fist, and the recording industry was firmly embedded in the fabric of the city. It's striking how quickly the industry grew during this time. One estimate at the time says that by 1963, nearly half the musical recordings in the United States were being made in Nashville. In nine years, the district had dominated the industry.

Still the Row had a down-home feel. People coming to Nashville to tour the city's musical hot spots were often surprised. They came to Music Row expecting glass towers reminiscent of New York or Los Angeles. Instead, they found a rather dingy little neighborhood full of run-down houses, dive bars and quiet tree-lined streets. The only "real" office building was the

RCA headquarters in those days. For all the power and money generated there, the neighborhood didn't show it on the surface. And there was an almost casual air about the way business was done in those little houses.

There were giants walking the streets in those days. Naturally, space limits the number that can be mentioned here—it's a story that merits a book in itself. There were producers like Fred Foster, who sank his life savings into the founding of Monument Records. The label was on such a shoestring budget that in the early days, Foster, his wife and their children would affix the labels to demo records by hand on the floor of their home before sending them out. From those humble beginnings, he would go on to a string of monster hits with Willie, Kris Kristofferson, Lloyd Price, Jeannie Seely and others, most notably Roy Orbison.

There were songwriters such as the legendary Boudleaux and Felice Bryant, who lived in a mobile home and a basement flat as they struggled to establish themselves. Times were tight—Felice once jokingly told a friend, "You don't know how tempted I am sometimes to throw myself out that window." The window, of course, was in the basement and level with the ground outside. During the early years, they collaborated on an incredible body of work, writing religiously every day. "You never see the ones that end up in the waste basket," Boud once said to a colleague. Their dedication eventually paid off, resulting in recordings by artists as varied as Little Jimmy Dickens and Simon & Garfunkel. Most notable was their string of successes with the Everly Brothers, as well as "Rocky Top," which was adopted in 1982 as the official state song of Tennessee.

There were groundbreakers and pioneers as well. One of the things that seems somewhat surprising is how many women in positions of authority there were along the Row in those days. Country music has often—and rightly—been seen as a boys' club. But some of the most influential figures in the industry at the time were women. There was Jo Walker-Meador, who started out as a secretary and who took over as executive director of the CMA in 1962, holding the position for the next twenty-nine years. There was the legendary Maggie Cavender, who left a successful career as an aviation executive to move into music publishing, working with "Cowboy" Jack Clement and Shelby Singleton. A hero to a generation of songwriters, she was one of their greatest advocates and went on to serve as the first executive director of the Nashville Songwriters' Hall of Fame in 1967. And then there was Frances Preston, who started off as a receptionist for WSM radio and who worked up to the vice presidency of BMI publishing in 1964—reportedly the first

A previously unpublished photograph of Patsy Cline taken backstage at her second-to-last performance, Kansas City, 1963. Her death rocked the country music world. *Joe Allison Collection.*

Producer Joe Allison chats with Frances Preston and her husband, E.J., at a function in 1970. For more than thirty years, she was one of the most influential female executives in America and a driving force during country's formative years. *Joe Allison Collection.*

woman to hold such a position in Tennessee history. Her career would last into the 1990s, when she retired as the CEO of the firm, one of the most powerful women in American music at that time.

And then, of course, there were the stars. It was a varied scene in those days. Some of them were just starting out on what would be long careers: Willie, Loretta Lynn, Merle Haggard, Dolly Parton. Others, like Jeannie C. Riley, would have only a single hit—although "Harper Valley P.T.A." would be enough to make her a legend. There were traditional performers like Roy Acuff and Bill Monroe, side by side with new innovators like Roger Miller and Johnny Cash. And some bridged the gap, like Eddy Arnold, who revived his career by embracing the new sound in his smash 1965 hit "Make the World Go Away."

Some, sadly, would never reach their full potential. Patsy Cline and Jim Reeves seemed to be linked by fate. Both of them had a short run of peak success from the late '50s to the early '60s. Both pioneered the new style that made them hard to classify—as at home on the pop charts as the country ones. Cline's biggest crossover, the Willie Nelson composition "Crazy," was recorded at the Quonset hut, while Reeves recorded a string of international hits, mostly at RCA Studio B a few blocks away. Of course, both met with eerily similar ends—Patsy in the spring of 1963 and Jim just a year and a half later, in plane crashes that were almost identical. For rock-and-roll fans, "the day the music died" came in Iowa in 1959. Four years later, country fans were left mourning two such tragedies: one near Camden, Tennessee, and the other near Brentwood, just south of Nashville. Their deaths would cast a pall over what was a very small community in those days.

By the end of the decade, Music Row had become a power unto itself, generating more than $100 million annually (the equivalent of $660 million today), and there were plans afoot behind the scenes to expand. Through alliances with city politicians, an ambitious scheme to expand 16th Avenue into a major four-lane thoroughfare connected to downtown was launched. The new venture, tentatively called the Music City Boulevard, would have meant a major expansion of the Row and—more vitally—the end of its isolation from the heart of the city. Plans were underway for a $4.5 million shopping and office building known as the "Music City U.S.A. Building," to be put at the corner of 16th and South Street. RCA, Decca, Pamper, Tree and Cedarwood Publishing—all had plans for brand-new headquarters or major expansions. Music Row was finally on the verge of becoming the industry center that had always been envisioned.

And then things took a major hit. A shift in politics took place on the Metro city council, and in November, it voted the proposed boulevard down. Worse yet, it converted the strip from 16th through 19th Avenues into one-way streets, severely limiting their utility to business traffic, a situation that remains today. Glenn Ferguson, the former representative for the district who had worked hard to put the deal in place, was outraged. "There is no question but that we had a commitment to these people…[which] is one of the reasons many of the businesses in the music field have located in this area."

The decision, however, was final. Overnight, the big dreams were dashed. Uncertainty over the future value of real estate brought on a big selloff among those who had invested in anticipation of the improvements, and there was even talk of Music Row disbanding, as labels sought more appreciable homes.

Of course, that never happened, although the early 1970s would be a low point in the area's fortunes. But Music Row would prove resilient. By the '80s, the building boom was on again, and the area would expand into something closer to the modern industry the pioneers had originally envisioned. The infancy of Music Row will ever be remembered as one of its greatest eras. But even greater days were yet to come.

CHAPTER 6

MORE THAN JUST COUNTRY

Elizabeth Elkins

As the Nashville Sound and word of the Music Row community spread across the country, more and more non-country musicians became enamored of the magic happening in north-central Tennessee. Three of the artists who came to Nashville to make records would not only change the sound of country music forever but also influence the art of songwriting for generations to come. Between 1966 and 1972, Bob Dylan, Leonard Cohen and Neil Young came to town, and the town would never be the same.

BOB DYLAN, *BLONDE ON BLONDE*

Columbia Studio A, 34 Music Square East

"People were sneaking to record in Nashville without letting everybody know that they were coming to Nashville," recalled Dane Bryant, son of songwriters Felice and Boudreaux Bryant. One of those artists was Bob Dylan, who had recorded the Bryants' songs "Take a Message to Mary" and "Take Me as I Am." Little did Dylan know that his pursuit of what he called the "thin mercury sound" would result in a record that regularly shows up when artists, critics or fans list the ten greatest albums ever made.

It's a record that takes your ears by surprise. From the wildly bizarre marching-band opening notes of "Rainy Day Women #12 & #35" to the sprawling heartache and anticipation of "Sad Eyed Lady of the Lowlands," the fourteen songs of *Blonde on Blonde* almost weren't recorded in Nashville at all.

In early 1966, musicians looked at Nashville as a songwriter's town—a country outpost, a hillbilly paradise far from the curious intellectualism of Greenwich Village or the anything-goes lawlessness of the Pacific Coast. It had hints of Tin Pan Alley for sure, where songwriters wrote for artists to record, where the artists themselves were more the vessel for the song, serving as interpreters of the words and melodies. Elvis was as far outside the box as things had gone. But the poets and madmen were on their way. It was good old boys versus the intelligentsia, and the result was staggering.

Dylan had just gone electric, and he wasn't sure where to go next. He began the sessions for *Blonde on Blonde* in New York, but he quickly realized that something was missing. He wanted to marry the words on the page with a new sound. He needed to trust the musicians to reach the level of his songwriting—a place where there were no musical limits. In Nashville, the studio musicians (often called the "Nashville Cats") were used to showing up, reading a musical chart without hearing the song prior and creating fantastic, creative musical parts to flesh out a song. This was very different than the way Dylan had worked prior. Dylan had recently befriended Johnny Cash at the Newport Folk Festival, and the idea of working in Cash's stomping grounds was alluring. Nashville recording strategy meets the free-wheelin' Dylan? It was a plan put in motion by producer Bob Johnston.

Dylan was hard at work on a follow-up to his critically acclaimed *Highway 61 Revisited* album. In the fall and winter of 1965, he worked in New York studios, looking for a "metallic and bright gold" sound built on guitar, harmonica and organ. Johnston had just left Music City for New York and told Dylan he might know a solution to his musical problem. He encouraged Dylan to try a session with a group of younger Nashville musicians, many of whom were influenced by rhythm and blues and rock-and-roll. One of those guys was guitarist Charlie McCoy. Fortunately, McCoy was in New York at the time. He sat in on a Dylan session and impressed Dylan immediately with his licks. "That's how it'll be in Nashville," McCoy promised.

It was enough for Dylan to travel south. On Valentine's Day 1966, he set up a session at Columbia's Studio A. It wasn't immediately right. Dylan tore down the permanent sound baffles separating musicians to create a more cohesive playing environment for the band. The normal three-hour

Bob Dylan in Nashville, taping *The Johnny Cash Show* in 1968. *Nashville Public Library Special Collections.*

sessions were tossed to the wind; players would take long breaks or even naps as Dylan worked furiously at the piano on lyrics and arrangements. Ironically, cleanup every evening was handled by the studio's janitor, a guy named Kris Kristofferson.

Henry Strzelecki, who played bass, remembered the band consulting a Ouija board about the album. "It was either gonna be the biggest album in the world or it ain't gonna do nothin'" was the board's curious verdict.

What *Blonde on Blonde* was when it was released in June 1966 was a sea change in the perception of Nashville. Suddenly, Nashville was the place to make records. Soon, numerous folk artists came to the city to make their own records. "It was like the floodgates opened," said McCoy. "It sent a message around the folk-rock world that, 'Hey, it's okay to go [to Nashville]. These guys can do this.' And it was after he came, that all the others came. They descended on us."

"[Dylan's] decision to record here in the '60s was a catalyst for many others to look at what must have seemed like an unusual destination at such a polarized time," said the Country Music Hall of Fame Museum editor Michael Gray. "If Dylan is doing it," he said, other musicians thought, "we should think about going there and checking out those musicians and studios too, in spite of its reputation as a conservative town."

Dylan would go on to make more albums in Nashville, including *Nashville Skyline* and *John Wesley Harding*. But it was *Blonde on Blonde* that transformed the city. Suddenly, the little southern town was a recording entity on par with New York and Los Angeles. It became destination for songwriters who played their own material. From Townes Van Zandt to Guy Clark, the Byrds to Joan Baez, Linda Ronstadt to Leon Russell, Nashville was the place be. Arguably most importantly, the record fascinated two Canadian songwriters with equally important songwriting abilities: Leonard Cohen and Neil Young.

LEONARD COHEN, *SONGS FROM A ROOM* AND *SONGS OF LOVE AND HATE*

Columbia Studio A, 34 Music Square East

Leonard Cohen looked for the muse all over the world. He found songs in a Buddhist monastery in California as he tried to mend a broken heart, melodies in the blue waters of the Greek island of Hydra and lyrics in the ice-river cold of Quebec's St. Lawrence. Perhaps no one else ever made New York City's Chelsea Hotel sound so haunted and romantic. But when he came to Tennessee in the late '60s, he did not know whether he should continue his career as a songwriter. He made his first record in 1969 and was not happy with the way the music industry worked. But his isolated time in a cabin near Leiper's Fork (about forty miles south of

The site of Columbia Studio A, where Bob Dylan and Leonard Cohen recorded classic albums. *Elizabeth Elkins.*

Nashville) produced some of his most powerful songs, including "Bird on the Wire" and "Famous Blue Raincoat."

Ironically, it was Johnston, the same man who convinced Dylan to try Nashville, who brought the Montreal-born Cohen to the city. Johnston is rumored to have cornered Cohen at a Los Angeles party, where Cohen complained that he had no desire to make another album. Johnston encouraged him to go to Nashville. The encouragement struck a proverbial chord for Cohen, who had originally entertained the idea of being a country songwriter. Johnston immediately put a band together, one that included a then-unknown Charlie Daniels.

They set up shop in the same studio where Dylan recorded *Blonde on Blonde.* There, with Johnston's assembled musicians (Cohen dubbed them "the Army"), they began work on *Songs from a Room*, which was released in December 1969; they later pulled the team together again for 1971's monumental *Songs of Love and Hate.* Cohen and Johnston would go on to make three albums, and Cohen became an instant hit with country musicians: Johnny Cash and Willie Nelson each recorded "Bird on the Wire," while Emmylou Harris released her own version of "Ballad of a Runaway Horse."

Cohen's time in Nashville, most importantly his time in the remote cabin (which has since been torn down), is the stuff of legend. Cohen allegedly opened the door without clothes from time to time, and one member of the band might have been growing weed in the adjacent creek bed. But for

Cohen it was simply another one of his isolated cells, a place to embrace loneliness and the muse—to create. Cohen biographers have argued that Nashville was the most important place he ever got "lost," as it gave him time to grow as an artist and songwriter—and record two classic albums that continue to influence songwriters on Music Row and the world.

NEIL YOUNG, *HARVEST*

Quadrafonic Sound Studio, 1800 and 1802 Grand Avenue

In 1969, Norbert Putnam and David Briggs opened Quadrafonic Studio, a state-of-the-art studio in two Victorian houses at 1800 and 1802 Grand Avenue. The two began their career at FAME Studio in Muscle Shoals, Alabama, each as a part of the famous Muscle Shoals Rhythm Section. They had also played for Elvis. They came to Nashville to play on sessions for RCA Records. Their goal was to focus on artists outside the Nashville country norm, and they soon attracted folks like Dan Fogelberg and Joan Baez (her hit "The Night They Drove Old Dixie Down" was tracked at Quadrafonic in 1971).

The artist who came next would bring in songs that changed the course of the singer/songwriter genre forever. It's a multimillion-selling classic album, featuring hits like "Heart of Gold," "Young Man" and "The Needle and the Damage Done." And it all began when Neil Young came to Nashville in 1971 for a performance on *The Johnny Cash Show*. Recording engineer Elliot Mazer was working at Quadrafonic, just off the main streets of Music Row. He invited Young out for a meal to tell him more about it. Young was intrigued, asked Mazer for a few musicians and told him he had a few freshly written songs he would be glad to try recording at the new place. In fact, he was interested enough to start recording that night. Mazer's usual players were already booked, but he found drummer Kenny Buttrey, steel guitarist Ben Keith and bass player Tim Drummond on short notice. That first night, they recorded several basic tracks, including "Old Man." Over the next three days, they laid down classic track after classic track, calling in James Taylor and Linda Ronstadt (also in town for *The Johnny Cash Show* that weekend) for harmony vocals. The recording style became the standard for Young's future recordings, with all tracks

Neil Young recorded *Harvest* at Quadrafonic Sound Studio, 1800 and 1802 Grand Avenue. *Elizabeth Elkins.*

recorded live in one or two takes, using a plate echo effect while recording. Young named the band the "Stray Gators."

Mazer recalled that the band was thrilled with the quality of songs Young brought to the studio. He played each song on an acoustic guitar, and then the band would discuss the arrangements, usually nailing a song very quickly once they began playing. Everybody played within a few feet of the next person, giving some "bleed" to the sound, which was a special part of the record sonically. The drummer, in fact, wanted to be able to see Young's right hand as it strummed the guitar, to lock in perfectly with the backbeat of each song. For Young, the guitar was the main percussive instrument at all times.

Word quickly spread around town about the incredible songs Young was recording. Players such as Teddy Irwin, Andy McMahon and John Harris each joined the recording at various times, playing true to the live feel of the sessions. But *Harvest* wasn't completed in that first Nashville trip, and Young returned to town for a few more days to add the songs "Out on the Weekend" and "Harvest." The quick recording style kept the recording budget exceedingly low for the time, just under $50,000. Mixing was partially done at Quadrafonic, with some in New York. But then Young needed back surgery, delaying the release of the record until early 1972.

Although his record label, Warner Bros., loved the album, the press did not agree. *Rolling Stone* famously criticized the album: "Neil's Nashville backing band, the Stray Gators, pale miserably in comparison to the memory of Crazy Horse, of whose style they do a flaccid imitation.... [The band] come across as only timid, restrained for restraint's sake, and ultimately monotonous."

Clearly, the reviewer had that very wrong. *Harvest* would go on to become the year's best-selling album and Young's most successful record, with two of his three Top 40 hits, including his only no. 1, "Heart of Gold," on it. In time, the album proved to be a milestone of the singer/songwriter scene of the 1970s, influencing dozens of artists who would later become hit writers. It is still a banner record for the sound of country, and Americana, artists.

QUADRAFONIC CONTINUED TO DEFINE a world of music in Nashville outside of country, including tracking songs for the Jackson Five and the Pointer Sisters and mastering the album *Phoenix* for Grand Funk Railroad.

Dylan, Cohen and Young set the stage for Nashville to diversify. But not everyone in town was happy about the change. Acuff-Rose Publishing president Wesley Rose began to worry about Music Row's future. "Apparently there are discontented people who don't like the idea of Nashville being the country music leader. Personally, I'm very happy with it," he said. "We have a few people in this town, who, because of a lack of understanding of country music, decided recently they want this town called 'pop city' instead of 'country music city.' They don't realize there are 20 pop cities in the nation and there's only one country music city. And this is it."

What Rose had wrong though was that non-country music had been happening all along in Nashville. Perhaps most notably was the scene on Jefferson Street, just a few miles north of Music Row. From the 1940s to the 1960s, clubs such as the Del Morocco and Club Baron were the center of a significant blues and R&B scene dominated by the Prisonaires. The scene was the proving ground for a young Jimi Hendrix. In 1962, Hendrix and bassist Billy Cox left the army at Fort Campbell together, driving south to check out Nashville's music scene. There they formed a band called the King Kasuals, and Hendrix earned the nickname "Marbles" from locals (who claimed he had lost his). Rumors that some of Music Row's best players, including Chet Atkins, used to sneak over to Jefferson Street to watch Hendrix play because he "could outplay us all" are still whispered across town today. Hendrix's innovative guitar playing developed as he watched other Jefferson Street players, and he was known to challenge them to guitar play-offs—he even lost a few times.

Unfortunately, the construction of Interstate 40 cut Jefferson Street in half, negatively impacting the economy, nightlife and music community along the street.

Back on Music Row, the genre-diversifying floodgates that Dylan, Cohen and Young had opened continue to spread. Over the years, other important artists set up shop in the city's studios. Artists such as Simon & Garfunkel, the Beach Boys, the Beatles' Ringo Starr and REO Speedwagon recorded next door to Columbia Studio A, at the Quonset hut. Jimmy Buffett followed Neil Young at Quadrafonic, recording "Margaritaville" there. And just off the Row, R.E.M. later made its first commercial hit album *Document* at Sound Emporium (3100 Belmont Boulevard). Although country dominates the industry today, musicians from folk to heavy metal, punk to bluegrass, classical to hip hop and all sonic shades in between utilize studios in and around Music Row.

CHAPTER 7

WORTH A THOUSAND WORDS

Brian J. Allison

I t has come to be regarded as one of Nashville's artistic treasures. Measuring an impressive six by ten feet, it has become an icon in its own right, a symbol of the platform on which country music was founded. As such, it has even gone on tour like many musical superstars and has been displayed as far afield as the Smithsonian Institute. Most recently, it served as a backdrop for Ken Burns's 2019 documentary *Country Music*.

There is little doubt that Thomas Hart Benton's final work, *The Sources of Country Music*, is a genuine American artistic treasure. Somehow, in those few square feet of canvas, Benton was able to put it all on display—the many people and places that created the sound of American music. The cowboys, the railroads, the old-time religion, the mountaineers and the African American experience. If a picture is supposed to be worth a thousand words, this one may be worth over a million, considering how many songs it represents.

But few people know that it also stands as a symbol of changing times within the industry. On a very personal level, the painting represents three men, each of whom was a visionary in his own right. And the painting will forever stand as an exclamation point at the end of one era and the dawn of another.

The story of this masterpiece really begins on April 1, 1967, with the opening of the Country Music Hall of Fame and Museum. Originally located at the north end of Music Row, the museum was conceived as a repository of artifacts, records and recordings documenting the past, present and future of the art form. And it was the library dedicated to preserving that legacy that was most dear to producer Joe Allison.

Born in Denison, Texas, in 1924, Allison was a product of the Great Depression and grew up dirt poor, living a hand-to-mouth existence. However, his natural talents carried him far. He first came to prominence as a radio personality and consultant and as a songwriter. From there he got involved in the business end of the industry, with notable success. He produced Willie Nelson's first album and went on to produce such greats as Roy Clark, Hank Thompson, Dick Curless, the Carter Family and others, including Bob Wills and Tommy Duncan's last albums. As a Texan, it was a fact that he was extremely proud of. He also continued his radio career and was well known as "Uncle Joe" to his legions of fans on Armed Forces Radio. At one point, at the height of the Vietnam era, he served as a reminder of home to those serving their country and had more than 40 million listeners around the globe.

Joe Allison—producer, songwriter and executive—seen here interviewing Lynn Anderson for Armed Forces Radio, circa 1968. He became the driving force behind one of the Country Music Hall of Fame's greatest artistic treasures. *Joe Allison Collection.*

One of the founding forces behind the new museum, Allison believed that it could be much more than just "guitars on a shelf." He was an advocate for expanding the collection to include fine arts to serve as a cultural centerpiece, as well as a financial investment. In his youth, he had painted signs for a living and remained an amateur artist as an adult; he knew firsthand the power paintings possessed.

It was on a trip to Missouri that Allison saw Benton's magnificent mural *Independence and the Opening of the West* at the Harry S. Truman Presidential Library. Allison's widow still recalls the thoughtful look that crossed over his face. "That was when he thought of it," she remembered. He later commented about what a shame it was that Benton didn't have a work on display in the state of Tennessee.

However, there were obstacles in the way. For one thing, Benton was semi-retired and not at that time taking commissions. Then there was the formidable task of convincing the CMA Board of Directors to back the project at a time when money was tight. "Nobody paid any attention" when he first brought up the subject, Allison remembered. The solution came after board member Tex Ritter, who thought the painting was "a fine idea," introduced him to Norman Worrell, who at the time was serving as executive director of Governor Winfield Dunn's art council. Worrell liked the idea and commented, "You know the government will pay for half of that."

Soon afterward, Allison made a pitch to the board of directors of the CMA, and Worrell explained that the project would qualify for a grant from the National Endowment for the Arts. Bill Ivey, at the time the executive director of the CMA, later recalled, "The NEA grant was critical to making it happen," overcoming some resistance from board members who were reluctant to back the project at a time when funds were limited. The final cost would be $60,000, with $20,000 provided by the NEA. As it turned out, it would be a wise investment on the part of the association.

Once the project was approved, the next task was to see if Benton would even take the commission. The CMA flew a delegation to Kansas City to speak to him and pitch the project personally. Worrell was to describe the parameters of the project. He was backed by some hefty "star power" in the formidable shape of Tex Ritter himself.

Maurice Woodward Ritter was born in Panola County, Texas, in 1905 and attended the University of Texas–Austin, where he embarked on an intended law career. However, while attending Northwestern Law School in Chicago, his career took an unexpected turn.

Tex Ritter, cowboy singing star and elder statesman of country music, pictured here with longtime friend Minnie Pearl. He provided the personal touch that helped persuade Benton into taking one more commission. *Joe Allison Collection.*

Since his youth, he had grown up on the "cowboy songs" of the late nineteenth century and performed them on and off at shows and on the radio. Gradually, his voice and presence drew him further into performance, and in 1931, he appeared in a hit Broadway musical entitled *Green Grow the Lilacs*, the soundtrack of which was entirely made up of the traditional ballads he knew so well. Years later, Rogers and Hammerstein would re-work the musical with an original score. It would go on to become legendary as *Oklahoma!*

From there, Ritter moved into film work, starring in a series of low-budget western films for Grand National, Republic and Universal. The films were aimed mainly at a young audience and proved immensely popular, serving to showcase his singing voice. Similar to Roy Rogers and Gene Autry, his film work was followed by a string of hit records, which led to him being dubbed "America's Most Beloved Singing Cowboy," a title that Ritter took in stride, although he was reportedly rather uncomfortable with it.

His recording and film career fell off in the late 1940s, although it was revived in a big way when he recorded "Do Not Forsake Me, O, My Darlin'," the theme song to the classic western *High Noon*, in 1952. Increasingly, however, he was involved behind the scenes and became a major player in the development of the country music industry. A founding member of the CMA, he was also a 1964 inductee into the Hall of Fame and a lifetime member of the *Grand Ole Opry*.

Personally, he and the artist had quite a few common interests. Ritter was an avid outdoorsman, as was Benton. Benton enjoyed telling stories and singing old folk songs and was a skilled harmonica player. Ritter was a walking encyclopedia of such songs and stories. In talking it over, it was agreed that if anyone could speak Benton's language and convince him to take the job, it was Ritter.

Before he left for Kansas City, Ritter asked Allison if he wanted to come along, knowing how much he admired the artist. No, the producer replied, as he felt he'd only be in the way. "If he takes the commission," Allison told him, "I can always meet him at the unveiling." He always regretted that decision.

Ritter and Worrell made their pitch, and Benton was receptive, but with a few caveats. Allison's original idea was for a mural depicting "The History of Country Music," to be painted in place on the wall of the museum on Music Row. But while passing a bottle of whiskey one evening, Benton made Ritter and Worrell a counter-proposal: what about "The Roots of Country Music"—with figures representing the lives of the common people who contributed to its development, "before there were records and stars." He also said that due to his age, he preferred to work on canvas and would have the finished piece shipped to Nashville for convenience. They agreed to both terms, and Benton took the commission. It was a project that he would throw himself into completely.

Like Ritter and Allison, Benton was thoroughly American, but he drew his interests and influence from a wide field. Born in Neosho, Missouri, in 1889, his roots were deeply entrenched in the fabric of his home state. He was the

The painting was completed in Benton's studio at his home in Kansas City. Today, the house serves as a museum to the life and works of the artist, seen here. *Brian Allison.*

namesake of his great-uncle, Thomas Hart Benton, one of the first U.S. senators elected from Missouri. In a way, this latest project would bring him full circle—Senator Benton had once called Nashville his home until a feud with Andrew Jackson had driven him to seek a new life in frontier Missouri.

Benton had studied at the Art Institute of Chicago, and like many aspiring painters of his generation, he had also studied in Paris. Following service with the navy during the world war, he settled in New York, where he resumed his career and became one of the leading lights of Regionalism, a thoroughly American school that found its inspiration in the day-to-day lives of the average folks who populated small towns and rural regions throughout the country. As the Great Depression took hold of the land, his work struck a nerve, and his fame began to spread. A prolific painter and printmaker, he became best known for large-scale murals in public settings, such as those in Indiana University and the Missouri State Capitol at Jefferson City.

His work is unique, consisting of heroic representations of typical American archetypes: farmers, politicians, laborers, cowboys and musicians. And he didn't shy away from portraying the ugly side of things. In his Indiana murals, for example, he portrayed several members of the Ku Klux Klan in full regalia—an organization that had overwhelming public support in the nation at the time. Controversial as the paintings were at the time, and ugly as they are today, the paintings are an uncomfortable reminder of a difficult moment in the state's history. And when he included outlaw Jesse James and notoriously corrupt "Boss" Tom Pendergast in his Jefferson City mural, he opined that corrupt or not, Pendergast had done far more to advance the state of Missouri than had his own ancestor, Senator Benton. He could be opinionated, argumentative, forceful and downright rude. "Tom made a lot more enemies than he did friends," his sister later recalled. But his talent and genius were undeniable, and those friends he did make truly loved him.

However, his approach to the new work was much softer, almost gentle in its admiration of the subject matter. Benton set out to portray the many musical influences that had come together to create modern country music. The fiddlers at a country dance, representing everyday music. A dose of religion from a gospel choir and a church on a hill. The often unsung are represented as well: a poor African American laborer strums on a banjo, a sack of cotton next to him. And two mountain women strumming a dulcimer remind the viewer of the contributions of women to the genre. Largest of all is a cowboy, representing the influence of western music. Benton intended the figure as a tribute to Ritter, whom he admired, telling him at their initial meeting, "Don't be surprised if that cowboy looks a bit like you." Benton delivered a work evidently close to his own heart: a comprehensive overview of the contributions that everyday Americans made to the most American of musical forms. Sadly, two of the three would never live to see it completed.

On January 2, 1974, Tex Ritter was on a visit to the Davidson County jail on business. He was sitting in a chair in the office when he suddenly collapsed. It was a massive heart attack, and he died before he reached the hospital at the age of sixty-eight. He was taken home to his beloved Texas and buried in Jefferson County. Allison, who had known him for three decades, was one of his pallbearers.

The CMA board voted to dedicate the painting to Ritter and continued to make adjustments. One major element that was added late was a locomotive as a nod to the contributions made by railroad ballads such as "Wreck of the Old '97" and "Casey Jones" to the American folk tradition. In January 1974, Benton wrote to Bill Ivey, "How could I have overlooked it? Though a late theme, I agree that it is too important to ignore." He went further, adding a steamboat to emphasize the music of the river hands.

It was a grueling pace at his age, but it was a labor of love and Benton took it on with his usual skill. He worked ahead according to his longtime friend John Callison, preferring to be a few weeks ahead of the schedule he'd set for himself. Nevertheless, he was driven by his attention to detail. The railroad train was the one detail he fretted over the most. Benton had a fascination with trains all of his life, and he couldn't stand to get a technical detail wrong. He wrote letters to museums across the country, trying to track down an original example of the model of train that Casey Jones rode to his death seventy-five years before.

On the bitterly cold evening of January 19, 1975, Benton told his wife, Rita, that he was going to "study that Nashville picture" in his studio. It was an old habit of his, to look at all the details and make sure that all was correct, as he didn't like to sign it until he was satisfied that it was completed. Labor of love or not, he was exhausted. Callison remembered how beat he was that evening, as he always was at the end of a project. There seems to be some confusion as to whether he was completely satisfied with it. Some sources say that he was still second-guessing some of the details of the locomotive and had arranged to travel to St. Louis to make notes in a museum there. Others, such as Callison, say that he had said that he was done and intended to sign it that night, indicating that he considered the work finished.

He was gone longer than she expected, so she went out to fetch him. And there she found Tom slumped in a chair in front of the painting. He had evidently suffered a stroke and fallen, cracking his watch and stopping it at 7:05 p.m., but he had made it to the chair before he died. Thomas Hart Benton was eighty-four. He had died before he could sign what turned out to be his final work.

As a final bit of irony, one of Benton's earliest known drawings, executed when he was nine years old, was of a railroad locomotive. In a way, his final painting had brought his life full circle. Sadly, Rita would only outlive him by three months.

Joe Allison left the industry shortly thereafter. It wasn't a pleasant parting. But with the death of his longtime friend and co-collaborator Ritter, it seemed to those who knew him well that what enjoyment he found in the field had died as well. He went on to a happy retirement and lived long enough to see the painting he had originally envisioned become a prized possession of the Country Music Hall of Fame. Before he died of lung disease in 2002, he said several times that the painting and the library at the Hall of Fame were two of the projects that he was most proud of having helped see to fruition.

The Sources of Country Music, Benton's final masterpiece, encapsulates most of the roots of one of America's truly native-born musical traditions. *Country Music Hall of Fame and Museum.*

"We have Thomas Hart Benton's last painting in our museum," he recalled. "The fact that it could be moved turned out to be a blessing." Indeed it was. If it had been a mural, it would have been left behind when the museum moved in 2001 and probably torn down with the original building. As it is, hundreds of thousands of people marvel at it every day at its new home on 5th Avenue South.

Its mobility means that it can act in a capacity that wasn't originally thought of: as a traveling ambassador for country music. The painting has toured the country several times and has been displayed at the Smithsonian's Hirshhorn Museum. It is considered the single most valuable asset in the museum's collection.

On a deeper level, the painting represents the passing of the torch from one generation to another. Ritter, Allison and Benton himself were all intrinsic in bringing American music forward from its roots into a new era. The painting is the perfect capstone to three brilliant careers. It is both a gift and a reminder of the giants on whose shoulders the next generation is perched.

And it serves a little advice from those who came before: when you're going forward, it's best not to lose sight of where you came from.

Chapter 8

Bubbles in the Fountain

Brian J. Allison

THE DATE: May 1967

THE SCENE OF THE CRIME: Country Music Hall of Fame and Museum, 700 16th Avenue South

Just about one month earlier, the museum had opened its doors for the first time. The unique structure—built to resemble an abstract representation of a barn—had been in development for more than seven years, and some serious politicking and fundraising went on behind the scenes before the city signed over what had been a small city park at the top of Music Row for use in the project.

On April Fools' Day, five hundred guests had gathered to listen as Nashville mayor Beverly Briley made a speech, stating that the land on which the facility sat "shall be a perpetual memorial…to past, present, and future" luminaries of country music. Roy Horton, the chairman of the Country Music Association, then used a symbolic six-foot pair of scissors to cut the ribbon. The crowd swarmed inside, enjoying cocktails while getting personalized tours from such stars as Minnie Pearl, Eddy Arnold, Faron Young—even an up-and-coming Hank Williams Jr. It marked a proud moment, when country had arrived as its own art form. By all accounts, it was a most sedate and tasteful affair.

It only took a month for someone to decide to have a proper christening ceremony. Late at night, a person or persons unknown strolled up to the decorative fountain and reflecting pool in front of the structure armed with a most unusual weapon: several full containers of household detergent. The contents were poured into the fountain, and it wasn't long before the churning waters started the show. The result was long remembered up and down the Row.

The suds quickly overflowed the basin, then the sidewalk, then the street itself, spreading a lovely white foam over everything and transforming the general vicinity into a slippery mess for pedestrians and traffic. It was great fun while it lasted and caused very little harm—other than a rather pricey cleanup and egg on the faces of a few folks. In a way, it was a bit of hazing that signified that the Hall of Fame had "arrived" and was accepted as part of the landscape by the very singers, songwriters and musicians who brought the albums to life.

It was one of the more legendary stunts ever pulled down on the Row. For twenty years, it was talked about and the identity of the phantom of the fountain debated. But it's only one of many such legendary stunts, pranks and examples of wit to come out of the area. Perhaps it's only natural—you simply can't put that many creative souls into proximity and not expect them to act up occasionally. And there's a rich tradition of stories to be found when you ask around—most of which are definitely not fit to print.

A lot of the clowning around was born out of plain old high spirits. As the old saying goes, idle hands are the devil's workshop, and in the past, there has been a booming trade in minor devilment in the area.

One of the more recent examples took place on St. Patrick's Day 2010, when the Row got caught up in the festivities as one of its largest residents went all in for the "Wearing of the Green." *Musica*—better known by many as "the naked statues"—which has stood at the traffic roundabout at the head of Music Row since 2003, has always been looked at uncomfortably by locals. Perhaps it is to be expected that a public statue of nine completely nude people—tasteful as they are—would be controversial in a Bible Belt town.

The naysayers must have approved that morning when they woke up to find that somebody had hidden the offensive areas with kilts and Irish leine shirts in a glorious display of Celtic pride—even adding armor, swords and shields for good measure. The local press complimented the pranksters for their "epic" stunt.

The culprits turned out to be a local musical group called the Willis Clan, who donned official-looking hard hats and work vests and gathered at the

The original Country Music Hall of Fame and Museum, which was torn down in 2000 when the museum moved to its current location. It became the scene of one of Music Row's most infamous pranks on a spring night in 1967. *Tennessee State Library and Archives.*

statue at 3:00 a.m. to pull it off. They actually filmed the stunt and posted the video to YouTube, where one can appreciate all their hard work—filming passing cars as they go unsuspectingly by while making comments such as "That butt's still showing." Since then, it's become a sort of a tradition, and the statues have been dressed in everything from their traditional Irish outfits to sports fan gear for the Tennessee Titans or the Nashville Predators. On one memorable occasion in 2011, the wind was so high that the kilts and other props were blowing all over the neighborhood. Seems nobody can keep the "naked statues" clothed.

But then nudity has always been a popular thing in the area. Take, for example, streaking and the late, great Glenn Sutton. He was a prolific songwriter and hit maker through the years, partnering up with Billy Sherrill and penning such classics as "Your Good Girl's Gonna Go Bad" and "I Don't Wanna Play House" for Tammy Wynette, as well as David Houston's legendary "Almost Persuaded." As a producer, he had a special partnership with Lynn Anderson, who also happened to be his wife. In 1970, he produced her biggest hit "(I Never Promised You A) Rose Garden," written by Joe South, which topped the country charts for five weeks and went to no. 3 on the pop charts.

Behind the scenes, Glenn also acquired a reputation as one of the wildest pranksters to ever stalk Music Row, known for his "zany sense of humor, madcap stunts, and outrageous behavior." Although their marriage ended in 1977, he and Lynn remained friends for the rest of their lives. In 2005, when she inducted him into the Texas Country Music Hall of Fame, she went into a bit more detail about one such incident. "You have no idea what it was like living with him back then," she joked to the crowd. "I'd get a phone call at two o'clock in the morning, saying, 'Somebody just ran naked down Music Row…*where is your husband?*'"

It should be pointed out that it was never confirmed it was Glenn, but if it was, he wasn't the only one who would streak the Row over the years. Case in point: one of the most talked about *au natural* moments took place on Valentine's Day back in 1996.

Those out and about that chilly morning suddenly found themselves greeted by a smiling young lady wearing cowboy boots, a cowboy hat and nothing else. One eyewitness saw her stroll by on Music Square East. "Yeah, I saw Lady Godiva walking around," he later told a reporter. "She was walking around butt-naked and she looked at us and said, 'Hi guys.'" A few tourists snapped a photo of her as she passed by Belmont Church. By this time, the police had swung into action, and three squad cars rolled in on the threat to public sensibilities. She was finally cornered in the alley behind MCA Records, and when told to cease and desist, she covered herself with her cowboy hat. Turns out she was an aspiring singer-songwriter from Wyoming and said she'd done it as a publicity stunt. Hers was a sadly common story in this town: lots of good feedback but not much attention from the higher-ups. With apparently unintended irony, she later told a newspaper, "I didn't know what else to do, and I really wanted to get some exposure."

She did, along with a ride in a police cruiser and a ticket for indecent exposure. Sadly for her, the gamble didn't pay off. Although it was rumored she was given a six-album deal by MCA president Tony Brown, it appears not to have been the case. Then again, at least no charges were filed.

She wasn't alone. Perhaps understandably in a town that thrives on fame, many of these incidents grew out of the quest for publicity. Stunts are nothing new, and in Nashville, as in other places where attention means more income, some folks will seemingly do anything to get noticed—and not always in the healthiest way.

Back in 1973, for example, when the *Grand Ole Opry* was still broadcasting out of the Ryman Auditorium downtown, a call came in just before the show was set to go on the air that a bomb had been planted in the auditorium. The crowd was quickly evacuated without anyone even suspecting something was going on. The bomb squad entered the building, and sure enough, it soon found a suspicious package taped to the bottom of one of the seats. It contained a tape recorder, and after thorough examination, the police eventually determined that there were no explosives attached to it.

They opened the machine to find a tape with a dozen song demos and a melancholy note addressed to Johnny Cash. The author, identified as a former El Paso deputy sheriff, said that he was going home to Texas, "where my wife and children need me more than Nashville needs another songwriter," and asked that the tapes be turned over to Cash for his perusal. In the end, despite the scare, nobody was hurt, and the *Opry* was only delayed by fifteen minutes. Needless to say, there are far more positive ways to get attention, and the stunt did not result in a record deal.

One of the unsung heroes of the industry wasn't a guitarist or a singer—he was only a fan. Finance for music people was always a tricky thing in town. For many years, Nashville's banking institutions were leery about lending money to anybody involved in the industry. One of the few who would take that chance was Clarence Reynolds of Commerce Union Bank, who became known as the "Banker to the Stars" for his efforts. He was known as the man who kept the show going and the tour buses rolling in the early days.

He also had a wicked sense of humor. Once he even got George Morgan, who was himself one of the most notorious pranksters who ever lived. George was on tour when his bus malfunctioned, requiring him to seek a transfer of funds for repairs. He visited the bank in the town he was stranded in and asked the banker to call to Reynolds to arrange the transaction. When the banker explained the situation, Reynolds asked him, "Is he a guy with blond hair?" And then he went on to describe Morgan to a T—height, weight, mannerisms, everything. The banker said, "Yes, that's him."

Reynolds said, "He's a crook. He's been pulling that same scam all over town. Don't give him the money," and hung up. After letting George stew for about ten or fifteen minutes—during which time he got so worked up that he nearly got kicked out of the bank—Reynolds called the banker back and let George off the hook. Eventually, he got his bus rolling again and left town with a scorched backside.

Songwriters are an incredibly talented bunch, and that many quick wits and clever minds in proximity invariably result in some classic stories and great lines. Some of these stories were immortalized in verse, as they were worked into songs. For example, in 1957, Jim Reeves had a hit in "Am I Losing You?" The title may refer to a dying romance, but the inspiration was far more prosaic. According to one acquaintance, Reeves thought it up one day as he was looking into a mirror and fretting about his receding hairline.

And there's the incredible Roger Miller, who was renowned for one of the quickest wits in the industry. "Did you like that?" he would sometimes ask an audience. "Well, here's a little something I wrote when I was singing that last one." He was only slightly exaggerating. But quick as he was, he also appreciated a good line when he felt he could work it into a song. For example, one of his biggest hits was "King of the Road," released in 1965. And there's a rather interesting back story to the line about old stogies being "short but not too big around." However, it's a story best told in person and not in print.

Other stories are more family-friendly but never made it into a song. Rather, they were told around the campfire whenever music folk came together to talk and socialize. A lot of the old-timers took great delight in cutting friends and colleagues down to size. Years ago, whenever a jam session broke out among songwriters, it wouldn't be long before someone started getting a swelled head. And that's when somebody would shout out the old line, "Hey man, play us a medley of your *hit*."

Some of these stories are nearly legendary and get better with the re-telling. It should be noted, of course, that these stories are part of the folklore of the music scene—whether or not they are true seems to matter little. Today, they survive as part of the vibrant tradition of Music Row.

One such example has been attributed to several folks, but most accounts seem to say it was longtime *Opry* star Stonewall Jackson. Early in his career, sometime in the late '50s or early '60s, he was on a tour circuit out west. There was no tour bus, just a car in which the band was piled atop one another, going from town to town on their way to the next gig. The story has it that Jackson (if it was indeed him) was dozing in the backseat when the driver pulled over near Truckee, California, and everyone got out to take in the scenery.

When he woke up and realized the vehicle wasn't moving, he joined the others and asked why they'd stopped. The driver asked, "Why, don't you know where we are? This is Donner Pass. This is where those folks were trapped for the winter and had to eat each other to stay alive."

"Well, hell," was the response. "I haven't picked up a newspaper in over a week!"

And maybe it really did happen the way they tell it.

The stars' significant others are also good for a line or two, especially when keeping an ego in check. Hank Thompson came up through the ranks of Texas Swing in the 1940s, and eventually he and his band, the Brazos Valley Boys, would outsell even the great Bob Wills. He went on to a seven-decade career and was still touring until shortly before his death in 2007. He was known for his honky-tonk style, as well as his flamboyant dress, favoring Nudie's famous rhinestone-studded western suits for public appearances.

At one particular function in the 1970s, he did as he usually did, moving into the throng to press the flesh and chat, while his wife, Ann, hung back at the edge of the crowd. She ended up standing with the wife of a prominent producer who was doing the same thing.

Her friend asked, "Aren't you afraid you'll lose him in the crowd?"

"Oh, no," Ann responded. "I just look up at the ceiling for the sparkles. Then I know exactly where he is."

It's a long and winding path you go down when you start asking around for stories about hijinks on the Row, and we can only scratch the surface here. But let's head back to what started this whole thing off: who *did* put the soap in the fountain all those years ago?

"Cowboy Jack" Clement thought he knew the answer. Clement, who was at the height of a wildly successful run producing Charley Pride, penned a little ditty that was recorded by the Willis Brothers. "Ode to Big Joe"

"Cowboy" Jack Clement had his own theory as to the identity of the phantom sudster. As it turns out, he knew more than he let on. Clement's Sound Emporium Studio on Belmont Boulevard, seen here, has recently been restored. *Brian Allison.*

didn't exactly burn up the charts, but it did identify "Big Joe" Talbot as the "insurgent who put the detergent" in the fountain.

Really? Joe Talbot? Talbot was one of the great characters of Music Row in its heyday, and one whose name is almost universally met with, "I loved Joe Talbot." He started out as a steel guitarist for Hank Snow but moved into studio work, making forty dollars per studio session as opposed to the ten dollars he would have made touring with a band. He went on to a prolific career behind the scenes as a publisher and executive. That year, he had just become the manager of the performance rights company SESAC.

His status would seem to put him beyond suspicion in the case, but Joe was friends with Jack Clement, and he did have quite a sense of humor. If anyone would know, it would be Diane Dickerson, who worked as Joe's assistant for a number of years. When asked if she thought he did it, she replied, "I think he had something to do with it, but I'm not exactly sure how much." She was determined to get to the bottom of it and made a few phone calls. There's more than a little Sherlock Holmes in her, and within two days, she had cracked the case.

The culprit? None other than "Cowboy Jack" himself. One of his two accomplices had spilled the beans. He said they brought a single box of detergent, but the fountain was too big and the effect wasn't very dramatic. So the trio went around the corner to the infamous "Murder Mart" and bought every container of soap and detergent in the place and dumped it in. This time, the effect was glorious. He even remembered that he was wearing a belt that he really loved that night and managed to slip in the goo and ruin his belt.

Well. At least for once, Glenn Sutton is off the hook.

Jack Clement was a great talent, a legendary promoter and producer who made everything he touched turn to gold. But it seems he was also the chief prankster of them all. It was perfect: nobody got hurt, it handed the world a good laugh and the sidewalks even got a good cleaning out of the deal. And he even managed to throw the blame on Joe Talbot so well that it took fifty-two years for him to be found out.

Jack passed away in 2013. His two accomplices are still around, and we shall forbear identifying them here. But they're definitely due the sincere admiration of anybody who loves a good joke.

"It was a small world," Diane remembered. "We'd all go out to eat after work at Ireland's on 21st [Avenue]. The janitor would be sitting next to the head of a record label." The music industry may have changed much since then, but one thing it hasn't lost is a sense of humor. And one thing's for certain: it's just a matter of time until the next epic stunt is staged on the Row.

CHAPTER 9

THE OUTLAWS

High Times on the Row

Vanessa Olivarez

OUTLAW: Living on the outside of the written law.

Buddy Holly, Waylon Jennings's longtime mentor, taught him to never compromise his music—he told him to always play what he felt. Little did Holly know that this lesson would serve as a map for the way Jennings would carve out his future and would create a unique and inspiring wave that would color outside the rhinestone lines of Music City.

Jennings was never the Nashville type, but his original projected path forked to the left, and Nashville became the "X" on the map that marked his destiny. The young singer-songwriter was living in Phoenix, Arizona, slinging drinks and songs at a local spot called JD's. He was discovered when Bobby Bare first heard his voice through an album he made in conjunction with a small label with an even smaller budget, A&M Records. Bare, on a trip through Phoenix, was turning the radio dial when he came across Jennings's undeniable country crooning. That song, "Just to Satisfy You," was taken immediately to Chet Atkins, who contacted Jennings and signed him to a deal with RCA. Atkins had found his new superstar.

While recording his first major label album in Nashville, Jennings met and cultivated the makings of what would be a fortuitous partnership with another rising star, Willie Nelson. They met while Nelson was tending bar at Riverside Ballroom and immediately found that they had much to talk about. The label, which had been urging Jennings to relocate to Nashville from Phoenix, was pleasantly surprised when Jennings broke the good news that Johnny Cash (who was renting a place at Fountain Bleu Apartments) had asked Jennings to be his roommate. The two singers, both on an extraordinary amount of pills, had an immediate connection through music and, according to Cash, "at that time, our love for chemicals." Jennings also befriended and began to write with heavy-hitting songwriters like Harlan Howard, a huge fan and supporter of the singer.

In the early '60s, most labels and producers were simply trying to make records that would sell—the pop and doo-wop records that seemed to only be gaining popularity. Feeling that the music they were making was too sterile and wanting to produce his own records, Jennings began to pull further and further away from Atkins. Nelson, who also felt a bit too boxed in by label heads and the powers that be, had retired from the idea of a mainstream country radio career and moved to Austin, Texas, in 1972. It was there that he discovered the Armadillo—a local venue that boasted "unorthodox" women, a decent stage and even massive crowds. Nelson reached back to Nashville and invited Jennings to join him and play the rowdy dive, and it wasn't long before the two began to develop a cult following of all kinds of characters. Soon, everyone began to follow in the footsteps of these pioneers, running from the confines of the boundaries of Nashville and into the freedom of Texas, where sex, drugs and a new "outside the lines" brand of country music ruled.

Burying himself in an endless hole of substances and depression, Jennings soon spiraled into the dead-end road of a drug-induced, money-pit tour. After some drug-related run-ins with the law and far too many close calls, Jennings found himself in the hospital in 1972, with hepatitis and totally broke. He had no choice but to try to renegotiate a terrible deal with RCA to get some money. RCA's offer did not meet the singer's needs, and he finally resigned to throwing in the towel. However, this rock bottom served as fuel for his fire—a brand-new start. Ready to quit altogether, the singer had a surprise visit from his drummer, Richie Albright, who convinced him that there might be another path—one closer to the feel and attitude of rock-and-roll.

Jennings returned, guitars blazing—dead set on a deliberate attempt to escape the Nashville Sound. He and his band stripped down the glitz and glamour of the old school and ditched the suits for more contemporary street clothes; clean-shaven faces were replaced by beards and gruff-looking mustaches. Jennings got a new RCA deal in 1973 that offered full creative control of his new signature loose sound and rough-and-tumble image. The result was something imperfect, something live, something real. A sound that everyday country people connected to. An album called *Honky Tonk Heroes* set the tone for a new breed of country music. Although the album didn't perform very well, it did begin to pave the way for a new subgenre to develop. In 1974, Waylon began chipping away at his next release, *Dreaming My Dreams*, at Tompall Glaser's beloved studio space, Hillbilly Central—despite breaking a clause in the contract that said he could not record anywhere but RCA.

In January 1976, a compilation including contributions by Jennings, Nelson, Jessi Colter (Jennings's then wife) and Glaser was released. The album, *Wanted! The Outlaws!*, sold over 1 million copies, the first album to achieve that number in country and western history. The album focused on story songs rather than the standard heartbreak and love songs. This was Jennings's and Nelson's first collaboration, but it would not be their last. Without trying, they were rewriting the laws of country music. Now that the four had formed an uncharted genre, the listeners needed something to call it. People need a name to go with the face, and that's exactly what they got. Thus, the term "outlaw" was given to the motley crew—originally coined by Hazel Smith, a publicist who looked up the definition of the word in an old blue collegiate dictionary and decided on the spot: "That's what they were doin'!"

Many "poets," attracted to this newfound country music freedom, began to flood the gates of Nashville—desperate for a taste of the money and fandom it promised. Writers like Shel Silverstein, Bobby Bare, Kris Kristofferson and Chris Gantry began to arrive in what seemed like an ocean of creative minds. Within this freshly paved path was a new way to do music their way. To speak their truth like never before. To make an artistic impact. This was the outlaw era.

Chris Gantry is one of the last remaining leaders in the outlaw revolution. He is perhaps best known for his song "Dreams of the Everyday Housewife," recorded and released by Glen Campbell on 1968's *Wichita Lineman*. The song peaked at no. 3 on the *Billboard* Hot Country singles. Gantry first arrived in Nashville in 1963—before the outlaw movement was even a thought in anyone's mind. Having battled autism throughout his life, music became his sanctuary, his way of escape, and he was a natural. While attending military school in New York, he became obsessed with the idea of Nashville and its pool of talented musicians. He would frequent the local record stores in New York, gaining as much knowledge as he could about this thing called country and western music. Then he

The "W" still marks the spot at 1117 17th Avenue where the DEA tracked down Waylon Jennings in 1977. *Vanessa Olivarez.*

Kris Kristofferson, Harry Warner and Chris Gantry (*left to right*) at the BMI Awards in 1967. *Chris Gantry.*

began to visit his city of dreams on breaks throughout the year in order to spend precious time where he knew he belonged. Pulled by the magnetic force of musical accolades, he relocated to Music City after graduation.

"I was fascinated that these people were writing all the hit country songs," Gantry explained. "When I got here the music business was only operating on two streets—16th Avenue South and 17th Avenue South. A little bit over on 18th Avenue, but not much. You could walk around and see all these guys on the streets. So, all of the sudden, I was bumping into them and meeting these people that I saw on the records in New York. It became real. I showed up here with my two songs and started knocking."

It wasn't long before he signed his first writing deal with Tree Publishing, whose roster included talents like Ronnie Wilkins and John Hurley ("Son of a Preacher Man") and Roger Miller ("King of the Road").

As Gantry's writing matured, he began to stray away from the comfort of Music Row's old guard and into the new outlaw wave. The popular country music of the time was mostly written by other writers along the Row and submitted or "pitched" to the artist to sing. However, there were some brave writers attempting to change the structure and sing about the things that mattered to them honestly. Gantry remembered:

There were the few people who were drifting into town that were seeking asylum in individuality. There was a contingent of writers who came to Nashville who wanted to be the kinds of writers who expressed only what they had in their hearts and souls—and were not willing to compromise their lyrics. Outlaw was synonymous with a term back in the day of people who sang what was true to them. It wasn't about trying to write songs for the music business to have hits. They didn't care about that, they just wanted to express themselves in the way that Bob Dylan and Woody Guthrie, and those types of people were doing. People who were writing what was politically, spiritually, and romantically in their hearts and minds. That's what they said was outlaw music, but it was just people being who they were naturally.

The new club included Gantry and writers like Cash, Silverstein, Kristofferson, Eddie Rabbit and Mickey Newberry. Gantry first met Kristofferson at a co-write set up by their publisher. Kristofferson was a bartender at a notorious local bar on the Row, the Tally Ho Tavern (formerly located near the current side of Curb Records on 16th). Famous for its "round table," writers would rally here for a drink after their respective daily sessions. Most times, after a few cold ones, the night resulted in an almost ritualistic trading of freshly penned songs. Gantry continued:

Tally Ho Tavern was like a Hillbilly archangel hang out. It was like all the people who were crazy in the world that loved country music—lived for it, died for it, breathed it, and had been doing it for years, ended up there about 3:30 in the afternoon. Every day. From Porter Wagner to Webb Pierce to the Glaser Brothers, and once in a while Johnny Cash. I lived in an apartment right across the street. These guys would come in there and hang out and talk music business. There was a bar and a huge round table, and inevitably, around 4:30, 5 o' clock, when everybody got a little loose, they'd start passing the guitar around and everybody would get to hear what everybody else was working on. For a young songwriter, it was like being in Shakespeare class. You heard the real vernacular of country people, put into story songs that were indicative of rural life and hardships on the road, hardships in marriage, love affairs, the beauty of alcoholism, the beauty of the road, the hardships of the Bible Belt and trying to live up to the word of God, and being crazy, and carrying a gun, and fighting with grandmothers who drove you out of the house with shotguns. That was real rural life. People sang about what they knew

Shel Silverstein, Bob Beckham, Kris Kristofferson and Chris Gantry (*left to right*) in a Music Row back alley circa 1968. *Chris Gantry*.

and that's why they had all the fans that they did—because they were singing to rural people who lived just like them and got every damn word they were talking about. That was country music.

Typically, after several hours there, they would move, almost in a mass, to the Professional Club—an after-hours hangout a bit farther up 16th Avenue, injected with a touch of sin. It was there that the artist claims he got the truest sense of what country music was in those days:

It had debauchery in the walls. You'd walk in, it was darkly lit, you'd always see some tricky blondes walking around. Women knew they were gonna get taken home that night by somebody if they played their cards right—and they never knew who they were going to meet. We'd all end up over there playing songs and such, but it got a little bit more boisterous. People were a little bit more loaded there than at Tally Ho. Sometimes fights would break out, but it was really great because, it put you down deep into the heart and soul of what was really going on in Nashville at that time. You got the vibe more in that place than if you were sitting in any record company talking to a producer, or hanging out with some songwriters in a writing room. If you aspired to be that kind of a person and write those kind of songs, it didn't get no better than that.

With the idolization of the outlaw mentality on the rise, drug experimentation was also at an ultimate high. The clean-cut image of the country music (which, of course, often carefully hid its own brand of rampant drug use in the '50s and '60s) of yesterday was quickly infused with a more rebellious spirit.

Free love and infidelity was more the norm than an exception along the Row, Gantry recalled. The use of "yellows" and "black beauties," which were amphetamines with a cocaine-like effect, was replaced with actual cocaine. Marijuana was also beginning to show up around town. Some writers believed that they needed to be altered slightly in order to write their best material. For instance, at Jennings's lowest, he once stayed up for nine days straight. Gantry remembered how writers got "the stuff" when they needed it: "The only way to get a little weed was…you would have to go up and get a matchbox full from a couple of the people that hung out in the clubs in north Nashville, along Jefferson Street. If you knew who *they* were, you had a connection."

Tompall Glaser's "Hillbilly Central" still stands at 916 19th Avenue. *Vanessa Olivarez.*

Shel Silverstein and Chris Gantry, 1973. *Chris Gantry.*

There was even a school of thought that perhaps a little run-in with the law could mean a serious career boost and a surge in notoriety. After all, it worked for people like Jennings and Cash. There was a romance to the erratic and senseless behavior of that rather lost group of musicians as they headed down a dangerous path. Glaser and Jennings and Hillbilly Central were the ringmasters. Looking like a western character, say Jesse James or Billy the Kid, was a big deal. Image started to become as important as the songs.

Although Gantry never got hooked on the hard stuff himself, he did have quite the brush with the law. When he began making money, the artist bought a farm in Fairview, Tennessee. The minute the dotted line was signed on his new purchase, he rapidly recruited his hippie friends to assist him in planting an acre of marijuana.

> *Everyone had seeds that they'd saved and had little hiding places where they grew it. We planted all these seeds and they started to come up. One Sunday, about 15 of my friends came out on a beautiful day in May. They all took off their clothes off and walked around the property. We were walking around the fields, and my neighbors who I'd never met before—stoic Church of Christ country people, came down the road galloping into the farm on horseback, and right into the middle of this torrid bunch of long-haired bearded crazy hippies. It took them a moment to see what was going on, and they wheeled their horses around and galloped out of the place. Not too long later, about an hour later, my water was shut off by my neighbors and people threatened to kill me.*

It wasn't long before the seedlings turned to huge plants, and Gantry's side business soared. However, someone opened their mouth about his oasis, and his property was raided by police, who showed up and started cutting plants down. "I told reporters later that it was too bad I got busted because it was the best pot that had ever been grown in Tennessee," he laughed. "Those were Afghanistan seeds, good stuff. That blew their minds too, so that hurt my case."

He dodged jail with a hefty fine, but the attention led an intrigued Cash to take Gantry under his wing. Feeling a great empathy for the singer, he invited Gantry to spend a little time at his cabin outside Nashville, while the heat of the controversy blew over. The friendship resulted in many fortunate events, including the legend recording Gantry's song "Allegheny Road." He also began writing for Cash's small publishing company, the House of Cash.

It was then that Cash gave Gantry the permission to make the record he'd always dreamed of.

"I immediately flipped out and said I needed a little bit of time to get it together," he explained. "So I jumped on a bus and went to an old friend's house in Veracruz, Mexico." There Gantry and his friend Jesus Amenado headed off to a peyote ceremony.

"I'd never done it before," he said. "The way they do it is very ritualistic. So I'm sitting in a circle with people I don't even know, and I get really violently ill from it. An hour and a half later, the world changed. Everything vanished, and I was in a total universe that was totally aligned to me. Out of that session, that experience, I wrote six of the songs for the album with Johnny."

That album was an experimental psychedelic acid country sound that Nashville had never before heard. It both baffled and fascinated musicians and writers alike. Cash and his wife listened to the album late one night, reporting back to Gantry that they didn't think anybody would understand it. The album, *Chris Gantry at the House of Cash*, never got released until almost forty years later, when Cash's son John Carter found it on a shelf in the old studio. Gantry noted:

> *Sex drugs and rock and roll are gone on Music Row these days. When you go up and down 16th and 17th, you never see anybody in the music business doing anything. You might go down an alley and see someone going in a back door with a guitar but, in the old days, you could walk around and shake hands with the stars. Now a days everything is filtered through interns and secretaries. Things are no longer accessible. Everybody who ran the business in the '60s and '70s were songwriters, guitar players, artists and musicians themselves. They got it—they knew what a songwriter went through to get something written and recorded. There was no competition. Then, it was all about the song. Now everybody gets a piece of the action. Even if an artist is a lousy writer, he's on the song. That's what it is most of the time. That's why there are five names on current hit songs. It's more like a committee than a collaboration.*

Still, Gantry keeps the faith and chooses to focus on the finite fragments left from the era of misfits—the stray dogs of vintage country. He says his favorite building on the Row is the Rhinestone Wedding Chapel (1024 16th Avenue, purchased alongside four adjacent properties in 2019, all slated for demolition in 2020).

The Rhinestone Wedding Chapel faces demolition in 2019. *Vanessa Olivarez.*

Gantry added:

> *I hope new songwriting vagabonds will continue to surface, and pave the way for inventive new sounds and genres. Something different. Writers have got to cultivate a deep understanding of themselves and some time alone to sit—to be uncomfortable—to get to the heart of what makes them unique. To create without the ideas of what they should create and make art for art's sake—and for their own.*
>
> *If you want to be a songwriter that connects with people, you have to get in touch with who you are. I think we've been put into a publishing situation where they are putting writers together to get a hybrid. We all know that hybrid plants are genetically weak. If you breed certain orchids with other orchids, they might bloom a flower, but genetically they are weak. Publishers now think this cross pollination of writers is what's gonna produce the great stuff. It might produce something, but it won't produce who that person really is. For my money, I want to hear who that person really is. Regardless of how well-written or poorly written. If the honesty is in there, you can*

pick up that they were trying to reveal something. That is what I want to hear. So my advice is to take your guitar and get a bottle of scotch and a couple of joints. Go, go check into a motel, turn your phone off and sit there for a week, sit there with your guitar and let things come up. Come up with something that's so indicative of your spirit, it's undeniable and nobody else can touch it because there's only you.

…As much as we want to give labels to songwriting, there's a mystical aspect to the process. How a person can sit down and make vocal sounds and put words into those vocal sounds and blow air into those words and create something that in a three-minute time frame you can break that person's world down—and you build it up again with a revelation inside that song. So that by the time that they are done listening to that song they are a totally different human being. They've changed. That's what songwriting is all about. We strive to write things that are gonna help uplift and change people from what they were, so that they evolve into a new kind of a creature. Those old songs from the '60s that were written in Nashville did that. They did that. In simple ways, and said those simple things. "Freedom's just another word for nothing left to lose" [from the Kristofferson-penned, Janis Joplin hit "Me and Bobby McGee"]. What does that mean? How many people thought about that line and had a revelation about what it meant, and it changed them inside? That's what music is supposed to do.

CHAPTER 10

MUSIC CITY NOCTURNE

Brian J. Allison

T here was a time when Music Row was a posh neighborhood. In 1907, for example, Mr. and Mrs. James W. Manier Jr. were listed in the social register as residing at 716 16th Avenue South. He was a wealthy wholesaler of shoes, and it was genteelly noted that the couple "receives [social calls] Wednesdays."

But after the Great Depression, the neighborhood fell into a slow, steady decline. The modest houses built with such care at the turn of the century eventually fell into disrepair as the fortunes of the neighborhood died away. Ironically, it was this urban decay that made the place attractive to the music firms in the first place—cheap real estate was plentiful. That is, as long as you didn't mind peeling paint and leaking ceilings. The famous Schnell Mansion was an extreme case of neglect but hardly unique.

Today, the casual visitor can walk the streets with relative safety. Music Row in the twenty-first century is far more tourist-friendly than in the past. The growth of the past thirty years has all but erased the landscape of the past, and it's hard for many tourists seeing the neatly maintained buildings of today to imagine how rough and tumble-down the same streets were at the height of the area's fame. In 1972—at the same time that Charley Pride, Tammy Wynette, Freddie Hart and Merle Haggard were churning out hits here—the Nashville Housing Authority did an official survey of the district. It counted a total of 296 residential and 156 non-residential structures. Out of 452 buildings surveyed, a whopping 409 were considered "deficient." One of these deficient buildings, for example, was a rooming house often occupied by Vanderbilt University students, who referred to it as "the Catacombs."

For preservationists today, who wonder why so little of the fabric of the neighborhood was preserved, it is important to remember that many of those who made history here never saw the buildings themselves as important—just tumble-down houses that happened to be affordable until something better could be built. As Harold Bradley put it, "All we wanted to do was to get started." It wasn't the sort of place to inspire much sentimentality in those days. And it must be remembered that the area wasn't exclusively devoted to the music industry—people had to live there as well.

It was regarded as "the end of the rainbow by hundreds of hopefuls who flock here each year," reporter Craig Guthrie wrote, describing the area as a collection of "plush recording studios and publishing houses, dilapidated rooming houses and beer joints," occupied by "music industry hopefuls as well as the poor who live in slum-like dwellings…medical technicians who work at the three [nearby] hospitals…and other girls and women, many from small towns and with limited…incomes who band together to eke out a reasonable [*sic*] comfortable life."

The corner of 16th Avenue and Tremont Street in 1972, showing just how tough a neighborhood Music Row was in its prime. *Metro Nashville Archives.*

As is so often the case, poverty and crime went hand in hand. Locals didn't exactly dread sundown, but Music Row long had a reputation as a rough place. Robberies, break-ins, prowlers and assaults were fairly common. Even so, what happened over the course of a two-year period in the middle 1960s was unusual, leaving a pall of fear over the neighborhood that would take years to fade.

The suspicion that something unusual was happening dawned during the fall of 1964. There was nothing terribly remarkable about Emmett Frank Elrod. He wasn't a country star or producer. He wasn't connected to the industry at all. He was just a pensioner, living a modest existence like many others in the neighborhood. At sixty-seven, he seemed to live a quiet life aside from a stint in the army during World War I.

He lived alone in a run-down apartment at 716 16th Avenue South—the same house that had once been home to the wealthy Mr. Manier and his family—and seemed to be alone. Investigating officers would later comment that after an exhaustive search they had "failed to turn up names of friends or even acquaintances" of Elrod's. He was last seen around noon on October 14, 1964, sitting on the front porch of his apartment house. Nobody noticed anything unusual until around 5:00 p.m. that evening, when a neighbor saw an unidentified man running away from the place. About the same time, other neighbors noticed that Elrod's radio was playing at an unusually high volume and continued to do so all night long. The landlord called the police in the morning, but officers got no response to their knock and noticed that a padlock had been placed on the apartment door from the outside, barring their entry. Somehow they didn't find this suspicious and left, saying that there was nothing further they could do. All day the radio continued to blast from behind the locked door, and as bedtime approached, the landlord once more called the police.

At a quarter to midnight, the officers knocked, but there was no response. Finally, they smashed the lock and forced an entrance. Immediately they saw Elrod lying on the floor, badly beaten and apparently strangled. He had probably been dead more than twenty-four hours.

Detectives found that his pocket had been rifled and his wallet taken, but nothing else seemed to be missing. Elrod had an impressive $12,000 in his savings account, but there was no evidence that he'd ever kept cash around the place. The trail ended cold. Other than the fleeting glimpse of the suspicious man running away, police admitted that they were stumped, and the case went cold. It seemed to be a random homicide. In hindsight, however, it appeared to be the first of a wave of similar attacks that would plague the neighborhood for the next two years.

In the months to come, there was a sharp upswing in the number of increasingly violent assaults reported in the neighborhood. At least two women were sexually assaulted. Another woman was slashed across the throat with a knife and left for dead during an attack but fortunately survived. All the attacks took place within a few square blocks on 16th and 17th Avenues. It was becoming obvious that a sexual predator was in the neighborhood. It seemed unlikely that the same person would have beaten Mr. Elrod to death over the few dollars he had in his pocket, but a terrible tragedy was about to strike that was similar enough to make many people wonder.

At 10:00 p.m. on the evening of July 16, 1965, Howard May and his wife drove from the house where they rented an apartment on 16th Avenue South to have a drink at Evelyn's Beer Tavern on West End Avenue. The couple had six children, including twin daughters only ten weeks old. They left the children in the care of his young sister-in-law, Wanda June Anderson.

Wanda June was only eleven years old. She wasn't from Nashville, but rather from nearby Joelton, just north of town. Her sister had married May, and she occasionally visited the couple at their home on Music Row. The fact that she was left alone with the children at her age seems shocking to modern minds, but the world of 1965 was a different place. Despite the crime in the area, few people at the time could conceive of a child being victimized. Bright and mature for her age, the Mays trusted her to look out for the youngsters on her own.

At about twenty minutes past midnight, the Mays pulled into the driveway and immediately knew that something was wrong. Both the front and back doors of the house were standing open, and Mrs. May heard one of their babies crying from within. A quick check of the room revealed blood on the bed where Wanda June slept. There was no sign of her.

After searching the house, May told his wife to call the police. As she ran up the outside staircase toward the phone, she happened to glance into the overgrown backyard. And that's when she spotted her sister, almost hidden among the tall weeds just fifty feet from the house. May grabbed a towel and wrapped her battered head with it. "She was beaten to a pulp," he later told a reporter, "So bad that I…covered her face and head so my wife wouldn't see how bad it really was." By 1:00 a.m., she had been rushed to Vanderbilt Hospital and underwent three hours of surgery by a team of brain specialists to try to save her life.

The house where Wanda June Anderson was murdered gives little outward hint of the tragedy that took place there more than fifty years ago. *Brian Allison.*

Detectives believed that the attacker had walked in through an unlocked door, found Wanda June asleep in bed and hit her with a metal pipe that was found at the scene. He then carried her to a shed nearby, but at some point she regained consciousness and managed to fight her attacker off briefly. He then chased her down and beat her viciously with the pipe, assaulted her and fled the scene.

It was an absolutely inhuman display of brutality, and it shocked the city to its core. Detectives flew the evidence from the scene to Washington aboard a specially ordered Air National Guard flight for FBI examination. The district attorney called in help from city, county and state officials. Governor Frank Clement even offered a $5,000 reward for the attacker.

Sadly, Wanda June passed away two days later without regaining consciousness. She was taken home by her heartbroken parents for burial in Joelton. The investigators were now looking for a murderer.

A pattern quickly emerged. In addition to the attacks in Belmont and Music Row, there were other attacks reported in the area off Jefferson Street near the State A&I College (now Tennessee State University). Due to his distinctive footwear, the suspect in those crimes became known as the "Tennis Shoe Man." The two neighborhoods were similarly poverty stricken and only a mile and a quarter apart. Investigators began to think that the attacks were related.

They soon found a promising suspect. A bouncer named Hughdon Mathis was taken into custody after the victim in the slashing attack identified him from a photograph. Worse yet, he had allegedly robbed and molested a cab driver in July and bragged to the victim, "You don't know who I am. I am the Tennis Shoe Man."

Mathis was charged with the assaults and robbery, but there was no evidence he was connected to Wanda June's murder. Nor did any of four other suspects pan out. By year's end, the case was cold.

But the attacks did not stop. The predator—or someone very like him—was still out there. For a while things went quiet. The police put twenty-five men on the case, working around the clock, and the increased heat probably drove the killer underground for a while. But it was only a matter of time before he crawled back out from under the rock.

On January 9, 1966, a bizarre murder occurred at a modest house on Nassau Street, not far from the scene of the "Tennis Shoe" attacks. A fourteen-year old girl named Reba Kay Green lay sleeping in her bed at around 4:00 a.m. when a man slipped into her room, fatally stabbed her once in the chest and then left. So quiet was the attack that her twin sister—who slept in the same room—didn't wake up. Her brother in the next room did and looked in on the girls. He saw something chilling. "I...saw somebody walking past the window," he told detectives. "They appeared to be laughing."

It was a truly bizarre crime, and whether it was connected to the others is still debatable. Like Wanda June Anderson's murder, Reba's would remain unsolved.

In the spring of 1966, the attacks on Music Row began again, always in the same manner. The attacker would break into a house where a woman was alone and assault her, beating her with a hammer and sometimes stabbing her as well. By August, at least seven similar assaults had been reported, as well as more than forty prowler calls. The only suspect charged was an Iranian exchange student from Vanderbilt who had been dating one of the victims. However, he wasn't charged in any of the other cases.

On August 3, a musician came home at 3:45 a.m. from a session and went to wake his wife by rapping on the window of the apartment they shared on 18th Avenue South. To his horror, he found the window open and his wife lying unconscious on the couch covered in blood. She was rushed to General Hospital in fair condition. Their two children, aged five and three months, had slept through the attack and hadn't heard a thing.

Detectives scour the yard searching for clues, July 1965. The murder of the little girl shocked the city to its core. *Nashville Public Library Special Collections.*

Little did the investigators know that just two hours before the attack was discovered, officers had made a breakthrough. Henry Daniel Wilson was picked up as a suspected peeping tom. He was a twenty-seven-year-old who worked at Vanderbilt Hospital and had a prison record for burglary in Kentucky but had not registered as an ex-convict when he moved to Nashville. Soon afterward, a telegram arrived from the FBI connecting Wilson with the evidence from an earlier attack—the one in which the exchange student had been charged. That young man was cleared, and Wilson was immediately charged in that case, as well as the one that occurred the night he was picked up. He denied all allegations.

Then the story got worse. Police Chief Russell Greenwell of Hopkinsville, Kentucky, came to Nashville to question Wilson on a series of attacks in that city. Delores Ann Russell, age nine, had been stabbed to death on July 3 while sleeping in her bed. That same night, two teenage girls awoke to find an intruder in their room who beat them with a hammer before fleeing. Wilson admitted that he had been in town that day, but no charges were ultimately filed in those cases, although Chief Greenwell said he considered Wilson "still a suspect" at the time he returned to Hopkinsville.

According to detectives, Wilson eventually broke down under questioning and confessed to the assault that had taken place the night he was arrested.

However, he later recanted, citing police coercion. In March 1967, he was tried in Davidson County Criminal Court on charges of rape and assault with intent to murder. On the stand, he made an unsuccessful plea that his rights were violated during his arrest and continued to deny his confession. The victim in the case testified but could not remember the attack or the nine days that followed it. However, the district attorney had enough material evidence to link Wilson to the attack, and after an hour and ten minutes, the jury returned with a verdict of guilty on all counts. Wilson was sentenced to a total of 120 years in the state penitentiary. According to prison records, he last came up for parole in 2016, which was denied. If still alive today, he would be seventy-six years old.

With his conviction, the attacks seem to have come to an end, but not the questions. Nobody was ever charged with the murders of Emmett Frank Elrod, Wanda June Anderson or Reba Kay Green. It should be pointed out that Wilson was investigated in the Anderson case but never charged. At the present time, nearly fifty years later, the murders still remain officially unsolved and still open. Over the years, several other suspects were questioned in the cases. Detectives have their theories but not much corroboration.

It's far from certain whether all the crimes were connected or whether they were the work of several predators. It should be pointed out that the victim of one attack was taken to Vanderbilt Hospital, and while there, she saw someone who "looked very much" like her attacker. Henry Wilson *was* working at the hospital at the time, but she described a white man with a thin face, dark hair and a smooth forehead, while Wilson was African American. Based on the description, another hospital worker was arrested and charged with indecent exposure. Incredibly, he lived directly behind the house where Wanda June died. However, he was never charged with any other crimes. The proximity of the cases and the similar method is enough to give one pause, but there is a distinct possibility that the crimes were unconnected.

If there was one culprit, did he get away and strike again? In 1969, twelve-year-old Kathy Lee Jones was murdered on Thompson Lane, her body found in a vacant lot. While there is little similarity to the earlier killings and the scene is far removed from Music Row, some theorize that she died at the hands of the same killer who murdered Wanda June and Reba Kay.

It isn't a pretty story, but it is a reminder that Music Row is not just an abstract, but rather a concrete part of the fabric of the city. The events of fifty years ago have mercifully faded now. Most of the places associated with these tragedies have fallen to the wrecking ball—as is the case with the scenes of the many musical triumphs that played out here. A lot of the bad has gone along with the good.

These streets were home to legends then, but most of the residents never sought the limelight. They were just regular folks working hard jobs and trying to get by while the music folk were making dreams come true. But sometimes the line between dreams and nightmares is terribly thin.

CHAPTER 11

POP-A-TOP

Tales from Dives and Honky-Tonks

Vanessa Olivarez

Although all are now a memory, for many years shady but familiar local dive bars and honky-tonks lined the avenues and alleys of Music Row as open-door invitations to the influx of hopeful creatives. Wide-eyed beginners and experts alike would enter as drunk and dreaming optimists—waiting to shake hands with their heroes, praying for that serendipitous meeting in some nicotine-filled neon watering hole that would change their career, or life, forever. It was in these broke-down palaces that legendary songs were heard for the first time, record contracts were secured and publishing deals were signed. Here are just a few.

KOUNTRY KORNER/TALLY HO TAVERN, 901 16TH AVENUE SOUTH

"I took myself down to the Tally Ho Tavern, to buy me a bucket of beer…"

This three-story red brick Victorian was a sight to be seen along the Row. Adorned with beautiful stained-glass windows, it sat as a staple for many years until it met its death toward the end of 1978.

In 1963, a rental property on the corner of South Street (now Music Square East) and 16th Avenue South was converted into a brand-new "bottle club" called 901. Bottle clubs were barrooms that would allow patrons to "bring their own sauce" and purchase a "setup" of their choosing (i.e., soda or lime juice, etc.) to help the liquor go down easy. During those days, Nashville was dry country, a long-standing Bible-Belt holdout from America's prohibition laws. Once beer was finally legal, it became known as the Tally Ho Tavern.

When songwriter Kris Kristofferson came to Nashville as a young hopeful, he landed his first job tending bar (paid), as well as singing his songs and allegedly flirting with blushing women (unpaid). It is said that this was the hangout everyone would rush to immediately after their writing sessions to enjoy a beer and share a few laughs. Even Johnny Cash was seen shooting pool there from time to time.

After the dive changed hands once again and was under new ownership, a brand-new name was also put on the sign. Some say the name change was an attempt to avoid the unpaid bills left by the last tenants, but either way, the building began its new life as Kountry Korner—or the Korner, as some called it. The Korner was a small room on the first floor, equipped with a few booths and tables and a half dozen random barstools. On occasion, outlaw ringleader Tompall Glaser would waltz in to have a beer and play a game or two of pinball, and you could find successful songwriters like Bob McDill and Billy Joe Burnette throwing a few back and talking music. Even sweet-voiced Brenda Lee was seen there on a barstool from time to time. Inevitably, a guitar would be brought out as a torch to pass around the room—for a sampling of new songs by old songwriters. The joint was operated for nine years by Kathy Jones, who was always armed with a can of mace for unruly customers, just in case.

The building received a blow it couldn't handle in March 1974 when a man named Bodene Hutchinson stepped into the restroom to give himself the final once-over in preparation for his role in a documentary on writers in Nashville. He was combing his hair in the mirror when the top of a 125-pound crane boom came barreling through the back wall, leaving just four feet between him and death. Water from the toilet shot all over the twenty-one-year-old, who thought a bomb had gone off; he hit the floor as soon as disaster struck. The crane was part of the equipment being used to build the United Artists Tower and allegedly just swung out of the control of Neal Ellis, a foreman for Concrete Form Erectors.

"It happened just like that," Neal remembered. "I didn't know anything was wrong until she [the boom] started falling." The gaping hole in the wall created by the boom was never really repaired and became a part of its charm and furniture until the Korner was forced to close its doors. Convinced that 901 16th Avenue South was nothing but an eyesore, WJRB radio owner Mac Sanders fought to have the place demolished, not realizing the weight that the revered bar held for so many songwriters. Sanders, later filled with an immense amount of guilt for killing their monument, held a two-hour memorial service on his station to honor the Korner. The service was complete with a eulogy, mourners and floral wreath décor. Speeches were given, and fond stories were told by folks like Minnie Pearl and Faron Young. The Korner may be gone, but it is most certainly not forgotten.

THE PROFESSIONAL CLUB, 810 16TH AVENUE SOUTH

When Tally Ho became too soft for some rebels in the howling hours, they would stumble over to the crazy arms of the Professional Club. The two-story Victorian house that once stood proudly at along 16th Avenue is now only an empty parking lot. This private club was a dark bar and burger joint, with smoke as thick as curtains hanging in the air—serving as a net to catch the brilliance of the songs hit makers would trade at the bar's famed round table.

Fights would break out, pickers would pick, industry boys would shake hands and deals would be finalized. Frequented by superstars like Harlan Howard, Wayne Walker, Mel Tillis and Mickey Newberry, the Professional Club presented an opportunity for beginning song scribes to learn from the very brightest in the ever-changing game of word and melody. While in a fight about money at the club, Faron Young, who had a reputation for arguing, was struck by a cue ball by a random patron from Indiana. Chris Gantry, who first met Johnny Cash here, received his first piece of advice from Cash while networking here:

> I'm twenty-one years old hanging at the club 1963, and Johnny comes in off the road. He's emaciated—skinny as a rail, probably weighed one hundred pounds. You know, from being on the road, living that lifestyle. I see him come in, he goes in the side room, and he starts shooting pool by himself. I just took it as an opportunity. I tiptoed into the room and watched him a minute; he's looking at me out of the corner of his eye, and I said, "Mr. Cash, my name is Chris, I'm new here in Nashville about a year. How do you become great at this? Not just a normal average guy, but how to do you get really great at this?" Johnny stopped playing pool and said, "I don't

Curb Records now sits near the site of the Professional Club, where Johnny Cash, Waylon Jennings, Chris Gantry and others used to exchange songs and stories. *Vanessa Olivarez.*

know you but the thing is, if you're a songwriter, I do know you. The only way that it's gonna mean anything between you and the world is if you be exactly who you are and write songs telling the world exactly who you are. Don't alter anything, don't change nothing. Just be yourself. That's the only thing that matters in anything."

MAUDE'S COURTYARD, 1911 BROADWAY

An empty building with a "For Sale" sign still sits at 1911 Broadway. Maude's Courtyard (opened in early 1978) was dressed in a more genteel southern charm than most of the Music Row hangs. Open for lunch, dinner and Sunday brunch, patrons would come to Maude's to enjoy an iced tea or a delicious cocktail in the warmth of afternoon sun. Named for co-owner Houston Thomas's great-grandmother, the restaurant catered to a family-friendly atmosphere, serving homemade salted potato chips, Cajun cuisine and even the classic Nashville "meat and three," loved by Music Row businessmen on hurried lunch breaks. This was a popular spot for industry heavy-hitters to sit and talk, unwind, refuel and make deals before heading back to the office.

Supposedly, it was at one of those wrought-iron tables that songwriter Harlan Howard first coined the phrase "country music is just three chords and the truth"—most likely at his favorite table, where he preferred the company of just a few good friends. Maude's was the victim of a fire in May 1986 and was forced to close for a few months. Starting in the attic, the fire took firefighters more than two hours to get under control. Luckily, no one was harmed in the fire, and its flames only reached part of the restaurant. Unfortunately, the popular lunch spot was spending more money than it was making and served its final dish on the evening of July 2, 1992. The bar was reopened as **Blue Bar and Rack Room**, a pool hall and live music venue of

The former site of Maude's Tavern at 1911 Broadway. *Vanessa Olivarez.*

the rowdier sort. Blue Bar was long rumored as the place to go if you needed a little extracurricular substance danger. Allegedly, cocaine was quite easy to score here if you just walked in and asked the right folks. It seems that this bar made the sharp left turn from upscale and breezy to smoky and seedy.

The Boar's Nest, 911 18th Avenue South

Sue Brewer was the owner of one of Music Row's most exclusive underground clubs. Brewer worked as a promoter for Webb Pierce, whose perks included the occasional joyride in his "Silver Dollar" Cadillac. A hustler, she also worked the late shift at another local bar, the Derby Club. After a long night of slinging drinks for the locals, she would return to her apartment on 18th Avenue South tired but seeking a night cap in the thing that made her feel the most joy: music. She turned her home into an after-hours hang for her musical friends.

Brewer welcomed singer-songwriters like Johnny Paycheck, Harlan Howard, "Cowboy" Jack Clement and Shel Silverstein into her "venue" with warm and open arms in the witching hours of what were sure to be memorable evenings. Soon known as the Boar's Nest, it was well run enough that George Jones later asked Brewer to help him open his establishment, Possum Holler, in 1967. After Brewer was diagnosed with cancer, Waylon Jennings gifted the gypsy philanthropist and her son with a place to live. When she passed away in 1981, Jennings organized a tribute concert for her, appropriately titled "The Door Is Always Open." It featured performances by Kris Kristofferson, Harlan Howard and Willie Nelson. In 1990, Brewer was inducted as an honorary member of the Nashville Songwriters Hall of Fame.

Bobby's Idle Hour (Various Locations)

The last dive bar on the Row, and arguably one of the most famous, was Bobby's Idle Hour, which closed its doors on January 12, 2019, but not without a good fight. Its first location was previously a Korean-owned convenience store called Kim's Market. Its second location, where the dive bar spent more than twenty years, was 1028 16th Avenue South.

Bobby's Idle Hour Tavern was forced out of this site in 2019 to make way for a high-rise development. *Vanessa Olivarez.*

As of December 2019, the bones still sit, like a headstone marking the finality of the old-school ways of the Row. Bobby's was embraced for its colorful spectrum of characters—the misfits who frequented the bar like harmonica player Janet from Another Planet and even the owner, who sported a beard that would rival ZZ Top, lovingly called "Lizard." Bartender John Distad worked more than 1,200 shifts in his five years at the institution and came to love each and every one of the regulars. "We have people from twenty-one to eighty-five that come in and play here," Distad explained.

With its numerous open mics and songwriters' nights, it was a true sanctuary for novice and professional musicians alike to try out shaky new material. Its aura wore an honest neighborhood-style vibe—with the laughter of the locals almost shaking the walls. Loyal customers and employees who supported its almost hallowed grounds for some forty-odd years rallied in support of the establishment over and over again until they were finally forced out when the property was purchased to make way for a mixed-use office tower.

"Bobby's is where everybody loves you no matter what. It doesn't matter if you're a great singer. If you have a passion for writing songs and playing music, this is the spot. When I first moved here, I found this place, and it became my home," Janet from Another Planet told the press.

As of publication, Bobby's planned to open a new location at 9 Music Square South, leaving hope that one last troubadour's paradise—where the misfits can return to create memories, share songs and buy a girl (or a guy) an ice-cold bucket of PBR—will return to the Row.

CHAPTER 12

TIME MARCHES ON

Changing Lanes in the '90s

Elizabeth Elkins

Garth Brooks and Shania Twain. These two names redefined "Nashville" for the entire world, bridging the gap between country and pop music, selling tens of millions of albums and creating income structures Music Row had never seen before. The '90s was the decade that New York and Los Angeles truly took notice of the money in Nashville—record labels that had spent years in small houses along Music Row built giant, glass-gleaming structures to house new departments, new staff and bigger bankrolls. Artists and songwriters who grew up listening to rock-and-roll brought that arena-style mentality to the genre. Brooks developed a meticulously planned stage show that was part Kiss and part glam rodeo; Twain's producer, Mutt Lange, mixed her Canadian twang with the drum and guitar sounds of his previous pet project, the rock-metal hybrid (and multi-platinum-selling) band Def Leppard. Songs crossed over to the pop charts regularly. Songwriters could make millions on an album cut or two as record sales soared. Publishers, managers and publicists were riding high as labels signed forty and fifty artists to new imprints and set the budgets in motion. Country radio was not yet corporate, and music was not yet digital.

By 1993, even the *Los Angeles Times* sensed that something big was happening:

> *The coast to coast popularity of The Nashville Network (TNN) and the*
> *international cable reach of Country Music Television (CMT), has turned*

up the temperature considerably in Nashville, where music and related entertainment industries in 1992 generated an estimated $2 billion for the local economy, and the Chamber of Commerce finally put the words "Music City USA" on its business stationery. The recording center and primary marketplace for country music since the 1940s, Nashville now threatens to become something much larger—perhaps a new cultural headquarters in the Great Escape from Los Angeles and New York.

In fact, one could almost call it country music's glory days. It's a time and place best explored by hearing the stories of those who lived it. Every songwriter, publicist, producer and artist has a slightly different version of how it all unfolded and why it went away so suddenly.

Tony Martin

Songwriter (Joe Diffie's "Third Rock from the Sun," Tim McGraw's "Just to See You Smile," George Strait's "Baby's Gotten Good at Goodbye")

What was the atmosphere on Music Row in the '90s?

You didn't feel like you were at the beginning of anything new—you just wanted to be what things were at the time, you wanted to write that. Writers who came in the 1960s didn't bring rock or pop sensibilities to the Row. They didn't have Bob Seger, Charlie Daniels, ZZ Top and Lynyrd Skynyrd as influences. It was no longer a fiddle and a steel guitar, even though we loved Willie Nelson. I grew up around the classic songwriters [Martin's father was a hit songwriter], but songwriting wasn't taught—you simply learned by doing it and apprenticing. You heard the hits, you heard the new things, you heard stuff that never got cut but everybody loved. I grew up understanding what a great country song is; it was in the air. But by the late '80s, we loved country but we also loved '70s active rock and rock bands like Kiss.

When the new decade started, Music Row was still a holdover from the early days when it was a hang—there were places you could go pop in and see people. It didn't have the corporate feel yet; there was no going to a front desk. You could hang and go in to publishers and say hello. All these little houses, and some of the biggest publishers were still in them.

What was songwriting like then?

People were not walking up and down the streets with guitars like people think it was—that was just gone by the '90s. In the '90s, you could pop into publishers' offices and demo sessions though. It was a free-flow creative thing where you mixed and hung out and talked. The writing started at 9:00 a.m., rather than 11:00 a.m. now. When we wrote in the morning, we broke and had lunch at places like Tavern on the Row, the LongHorn Steakhouse or Maude's—I called them all the "Music City Cafeteria"—and you saw other people and artists who were writing that day. You could still find Harland Howard in the courtyard at Maude's. There was a connectedness. Think of all the writers as molecules bumping into each other and creating friction—you wrote, talked about life, went to lunch, wrote more. Songs could be deeper and more thought out; you didn't necessarily get them done in a day. You wanted to be on the Row; if you weren't, you were on an island somewhere, you might as well be in another state.

Former site of the LongHorn Steakhouse at 110 Lyle Avenue, the lunchtime hang for songwriters and music industry bigwigs. *Elizabeth Elkins.*

You could make a good living on album cuts. I made more money in mechanicals [album sales] than the performance royalties [radio broadcast payments]. The rising tide lifts all boats—that's how the Row used to feel. If somebody had a hit with a song, it was selling the albums so everybody was rooting for it. Artists wanted to make an album like a show, to spend forty minutes with their fans. It was never just about the radio single.

Did Music Row go global?

Definitely. It was all about selling records. The older songwriters felt like things went pop, but it really didn't—it was just suddenly massive sales. It was the best-selling genre of music all of a sudden. A dot meant gold, a diamond meant platinum, then diamond with numbers for double, triples. If you look at album sales in the '90s, it's all dots and diamonds and exponential numbers.

When did the boom stop and why?

File-sharing. Napster ushered in the idea that you won't own creative content. It's the innovators dilemma—you want to make the highest quality for highest profit. But in music, somebody came in and said they could put ten thousand songs on a stick of gum, well, that is probably the biggest paradigm shift we hit in the music business. Music became à la carte.

I went to Washington over file sharing. For a while, it was a thing a few people did; you could see it was a problem, but the powers that be wanted to hang on and not allow it to come up. The first part of it the labels tried to squash it and fight it. But then it exploded. It was clear real quick that people were finding new music on Napster and then went and bought the album. Cassettes would degrade; digital didn't. When has any time fighting technology won in civilization? The big problem was that music was suddenly free. In a sense, music is free—you can sing it all you want, but the production of it isn't. But we held out; we knew if people really loved a song, they would buy it at the time.

What is the legacy of '90s country music?

Well, you can hear it still today, artists like Luke Combs are trying to sound '90s—it's classic today. But that boom also changed things. I didn't sit in a room writing "Third Rock from the Sun" thinking it would ever be on the radio. When the dollars get bigger, you take less risks. That's why we have vanilla ice cream—the most people like it. The bigger the audience for Nashville got, the more you had to narrow down what you do. Over time, we lost more and more parts.

MARK NESLER

Songwriter (George Strait's "Living and Living Well," Tim McGraw's "Just to See You Smile," Aaron Tippin's "For You I Will") Guitarist (Tracy Byrd) Artist (Elektra Records)

What was the atmosphere on Music Row in the '90s?

It was community—if you knew somebody was cutting a session, you popped in. You could listen to songs being tracked. I remember one morning I was going to write at MCA, I heard a song playing in a car that was a song I had written. The guy rolled down the window and said, "Hey man I'm Darryl Worley—come in and take a listen." You never knew what was going to happen around the Row because we were all in such close quarters, and there was so much creativity.

What was songwriting like then?

I learned what a hit song was and what it should sound like. You knew because of the emotion. It made you cry or laugh. That has changed the most. At the height of my career, when you played the Bluebird you played your saddest song—you wanted to break the audience down—but now a song like "I Miss My Friend" is a downer. That changing is the most difficult thing to navigate as a writer. You knew where the bar was when you moved to town; it was intimidating. But at the time, songs could pay mortgages and send kids to college.

As writers, we grew up listening to Merle Haggard and George Jones, but also the Eagles. You add Garth [Brooks] into that and suddenly a younger demographic embraced country. We didn't lose what the songwriting pioneers brought in. We didn't lose the older audience—we just added to it.

And co-writing was almost always just two people. A lot of the great songs were even by just one person.

Did Music Row go global?

Country reached a whole other plateau in popularity. It was selling more records than the industry had ever seen. Tracy Byrd—who was never as big as Alan Jackson or Tim McGraw—he sold double platinum. It was crazy how many records were being sold. Mark Willis sold gold and had an eight-week no. 1—and that wasn't good enough for his record label, he got dropped. Artists like Garth [Brooks] were pushing the needle, and his show was cool—because it had rock-and-roll in it.

Trey Bruce

Songwriter (Shelby Lynne's "Things Are Tough All Over," Randy Travis's "Look Heart, No Hands," Diamond Rio's "How Your Love Makes Me Feel")

What was the atmosphere on Music Row in the '90s?

Things started going platinum, things just took off. It never occurred to us as writers that it wasn't exciting to have an album cut, though nowadays that's a failure. By the end of the decade, most of us had so much money because record sales and radio airplay were both massive. You couldn't have scripted my luck better on the timing—it was insane. I had four country songs. I was in a rock band, and my singer knew an engineer at MCA Publishing. Everyone else told me I needed to write more. I got a meeting at MCA, played my four songs, got a co-write, which got recorded, and then I got a deal. I still delivered pizzas for a while on my $8,000-a-year advance. My boss raised that advance to $10,000 a year when I delivered a pizza to his house. But those advances were how you stayed alive. The royalties were how you got rich.

Trey Bruce recording with guitarist J.T. Corenflos in the mid-'90s, most likely at OmniSound Studios on Division Street. *Trey Bruce.*

What was songwriting like then?

You could still run over to a record label with your guitar and play a new song for them. You didn't have to have a big demo recording. My first no. 1 was a live guitar vocal cassette recording. I always wrote on the Row. You would call in and book a room at your publishing house—first-come, first-serve. It was the same way with the studio: we could finish a song and go right in and record it. The rooms were tiny, maybe a chair or a table, and you could hear people in the other rooms. We started writing at 9:00 or 10:00 a.m. Everybody took lunch breaks, [and] you would always run into lots of other writers at the LongHorn or Sunset Grill—then you went back to the room and finished. It was very social.

Music Row was sprung with excitement. Communication about who was cutting what and when was free-flowing. We knew that most artists in town would not be writing their own records—they needed us. Sammy B's and other restaurants on the Row were full of life. At Sammy B's upstairs at the tables in the afternoons you would find writers writing songs. There was a lot of senseless ribaldry there until the early evening.

You would see real songwriters with massive hits hanging out in bars at the end of the day.

Did Music Row go global?

Yes, and I can explain the blow-up now but not then (because we had no internet to see what was happening outside of town). I remember going to Los Angeles early on and there was no reception; they treated us like people from Nashville who likely rode horses to work. But then there was Shania [Twain] and Diamond Rio and Garth [Brooks] and the Dixie Chicks. Suddenly things got exotic and pop country. And then we were hip. As writers on Music Row, we didn't think we were hip, but they proved us wrong. Suddenly country music concerts were super stadium-sized. There were cables and acrobatics and huge ticket sales, which caused the record sales to get even bigger. Albums would sell 4 million copies off a first single and 10 million by a second single [for comparison, a country album rarely sells more than 100,000 copies in 2019].

When did the boom stop and why?

I went to my first meeting on Napster in 1999. I wasn't smart enough to know what I was at, but a co-writer of mine knew something wasn't right and he brought me to the meeting. At that point, sales were through the roof, but at that meeting I knew something changed. The attitude was that "we can beat them, we don't need to partner with them"—not much of an official business plan, but that is how it felt. We definitely didn't open our arms to try to be partners; we tried to stomp it out. It went downhill from there until summer of 2012, which I think is when it bottomed out. That was the same summer Spotify came here and answered the problem of iTunes killing the album. That's when publishing hit an all-time low. Every answer we got was a great answer, but we didn't realize it would kill us.

PAM LEWIS

Manager (Garth Brooks, Trisha Yearwood)
Publicist (MTV, Dolly Parton, Alabama, Kenny Rogers)

Did Music Row go global?

Country music has always been global. There have always been fans internationally, and we began with Garth Brooks's first single developing that market. What had happened often was artists would succeed in the States and have a good run, then develop the other markets. We developed simultaneously by hiring radio promotions and PR in the UK. The Country Music Association (CMA) even had an office in London; they don't anymore. There were always artists who had an international following. Charley Pride, Don Williams, Boxcar Willie, Johnny Cash, Dolly Parton, George Hamilton IV, George Strait—they all had careers overseas. Bob Saporiti headed up the international department of Warner Bros. here in town for many years. We always had an international stage at Fan Fair, and there were festivals throughout Europe and Canada, even Japan. More folk artists like John Prine and Nanci Griffith also toured internationally. The '90s were just a big extension of that.

How did you end up working with Garth Brooks and Trisha Yearwood?

I worked with both of them early in their careers, getting them both their first record deals and platinum records and eventually their no. 1s. I remember both of them were singing demos for extra cash around the Row, and Garth came back to the office raving about this woman named Trisha whom he sang with. He marveled at how their voices blended. I knew then he was smitten.

What was the atmosphere on Music Row in the '90s?

Music Row was like a big campus. It has always been about proximity. You can walk everywhere after all. I think we all had a healthy competition, but people got excited for the success of others in the business and for just really good songs, lyrics and production. Business was very collaborative and very social. You could catch Harlan Howard at Maude's every afternoon sitting

Pam Lewis and Garth Brooks celebrate big sales in the '90s. *PLA Media*.

at the bar. Tavern on the Row (affectionately known then as "Tavern Full of Blow") was hoppin' and later on the LongHorn and Slice of Life were the hangs. There were block parties, and you could call the *Opry* and ask for backstage passes if you knew the guards or staff without any problems. It was a real sense of community.

Tavern on the Row, Bobby's Idle Hour, the old Warner Bros., building, the Combine building, the Quonset hut and all of the Ray Stevens properties. There were so many awesome places. Many of those were National Historic Register–eligible buildings, and it breaks my heart every time one is torn down.

When did the boom stop and why?

I think when the budgets increased exponentially when studios went digital, the economies of scale changed. With the cost of digital recording usually in the six figures, artists needed to sell a lot more albums to recoup and make any money. So, while the fidelity improved with digital, the recording costs in turn went up. But fans could now buy CDs and burn copies for their friends without compromising quality. This also impacted sales. And then there was Napster, which we tried to fight rather than work with. We failed.

The method of distributing music had changed forever, and people stopped buying music which they could stream and share for free. There was so much music being made that it was fighting for airtime on the charts, and the cost of radio promotion escalated. Fans now have the option to choose the individual songs they like and, in essence, create their own playlists—albums turned into filler. It was truly a boom and bust.

What is the legacy of '90s country music?

Damn good songs and music. Even if we haven't held up, the music has.

PAT HIGDON

Publisher, Universal Music Group, Windswept and Patrick Joseph Music (Deana Carter's "Strawberry Wine," John Michael Montgomery's "I Can Love You Like That," Trisha Yearwood's "Walkaway Joe" and "XXX's and OOO's")

Publishers pitch songwriters' songs to the artists and their representatives. What was this song "plugging" like in the '90s?

Things here were a lot different than what they are today in every aspect. There were no artist/writers. Artists needed writers. The proliferation of people trying to write their own records wasn't there. We had twenty-five labels and therefore a lot more places to go with songs. There were a lot more releases. Each new album had six or seven outside songs [songs from outside a label's or artist's close circle] at least. There were less co-writers. A three-way was an exception to the rule. A lot of writers wrote by themselves and had hits.

Writers used to work more for themselves. I didn't use to schedule their writes for them. They found their own writers, set up things for themselves. My job back then was 75 percent pitching songs and playing songs for artists and producers and 25 percent the administrative stuff. The legendary writers like Hugh Prestwood and Dave Loggins—they were both really bringing something to it. Labels and artists fought over their songs.

Songs could have a very different path than they do today. An example is Randy Travis's "On the Other Hand," though it's right before the '90s. The writers [Paul Overstreet and Don Schlitz] wanted somebody like George Jones or Merle Haggard to cut it. I didn't have the power to get it to those artists at the time, but I saw Randy Travis play at the Nashville Palace and sent it to his people. He put it out as his first single, but it didn't take off so they pulled it. In the meantime, Keith Whitely had cut it; I had to go talk them out of putting it out as a single so it could have a chance later in Randy's career, which it did, going no. 1. That kind of thing doesn't happen anymore because songs are so easily available online. Video also changed it—once it's out now, nobody else records it, and if it fails the first time, it's over.

What was the atmosphere on Music Row in the '90s?

It wasn't like new labels were coming to town. There was just some splintering of labels and more promotion teams. The power of the music we were making here became more of the forefront in other places. A lot of things were more communal. There weren't as many silos where everybody kept their business in one group of people. Not as many camps. As far as getting recognition from other publishers and writers, you didn't have to fight for that. It was more of a sharing, caring atmosphere. You knew a lot of writers from other companies, you heard songs of theirs and lauded their writing efforts on a regular basis. I would go into pitch meetings and I'd heard another writer's songs, and I would say, "You ought to get this song for your artist." There was such a community effort to get songs recorded. All of the labels were still on the Row in little houses; nobody had left for downtown or the Gulch yet.

There were more women on the radio then—Pam Tills, Trisha Yearwood, Deana Carter. I don't think radio was as scrutinizing as they have been in the last few years. I don't think the concept of our listeners "tuning out women" had filtered into the marketplace. If you were shopping an act, you didn't even think about it being male or female.

Deana Carter and Pat Higdon at a no. 1 party at BMI, 10 Music Square South, around 1996. *Pat Higdon.*

The LongHorn and Maude's were the watering holes. All the big publishers and label guys sat at the bar. There was an O'Charleys on 21st Avenue—that was lunch hang for publishers. The Row has just changed. There used to be block parties all the time, sponsored by labels. You don't see much of that now.

Did Music Row go global?

I had some big hits, but we didn't make money internationally—I think the explosion happened when Soundscan [a sales tracking system invented in 1991 and used as the sales source for the *Billboard* music charts] came along, and folks in New York and Los Angeles discovered how many units some of these acts were selling. Fifteen labels here had platinum-selling acts or better. I personally think the numbers were already there, but New York and LA hadn't taken notice prior. It was that class of 1989 artists, the new guys—Garth Brooks, Clint Black, Alan Jackson. The '80s acts were declining as the Urban Cowboy era ended. But these great new traditionalists showed up, and along with them came the new eyes and new ears.

Garth found a great core group of writers and a great core group of songs. He had Alan Reynolds, a great song person, working with him. A lot of things worked around that. He was a great self-promoter and visionary of what he wanted to do. He and his songs stepped outside the bounds of what people were used to. "The Thunder Rolls" and "Friends in Low Places" were different, but they fit in the format. He benefited from a strong marketing vision, and a lot came from him. I played songs for Shania [Twain] a few times, and what she was looking for for her first record wasn't anything like what she ended up doing for following records. Early on, Mutt Lange wasn't even in the production vision. When they teamed up, he dramatically tailored a sound around her. It was a more worldly sound that could be marketed on a global basis.

When did the boom stop and why?

I didn't feel the change immediately at the end of the '90s. It was a few years after. I went to Universal in 1999, and there was a point in time a year or two later where I was actually involved in a discussion with the digital marketing people at Universal. And we were talking about the effects Napster had and starting to talk about new digital uses, but it took a minute for things to catch up. In mid-2000s, we were still evaluating song catalogues without digital as a barometer of value. But the change came swiftly. As publishers, we weren't digitally inclined like a label was—we weren't lobbying and trying to discover what made digital sources valuable to us. We were still living off the old income mentality—including how we set up our budgets. As things started to evolve, and the sales income went dramatically down, your budgets for writers and staff was stretched. There were so many more writers who had deals. You didn't need a hit a year or a few huge singles to make advances back, so you could have writers that limped along without album cuts and you made enough money to keep them in your fold until they had a hit. That changed to where you were under the gun to generate activity and income as soon as you signed a writer. Deals changed—money went down for the writers after that. You couldn't speculate money. It changed the ability to make long-term firm deals—you had to use option deals so you could get out if you had too much money on the table.

What were some of your favorite places on Music Row then?

Well, there was a house where the Virgin Hotel is now [see chapter 13]. I took the elderly couple living there coffee and doughnuts every day to try to buy that beautiful old house, but the son had the property in a trust and the house is now gone. There were some shotgun apartments where Starstruck Entertainment is now; they were not in good shape, but the legacy of the writers that lived there and wrote there was massive. They seemed like historic ground. I also miss the Kountry Korner—you could walk over there on a nice day and they would have two picnic tables out back, and you would see everybody out playing songs for whoever was there. New writers and hit writers would play and drink beer.

What is the legacy of '90s country music?

It was definitely a period of time that established the country music marketplace as a global marketplace by the end of the decade. I think of all the vintage rock acts that are still touring and how they were established by the '70s, and that gave them a base to tour forever. I think the '90s did that for Nashville. There were a lot of great stars and careers that started then, and people remember it.

PORTER HOWELL

Songwriter and Guitarist, Little Texas

When did you realize you were a part of something big in the '90s?

I came to Music Row from East Texas through Belmont College, where I was a guitar major. That led me to Opryland, where most of Little Texas started. We signed a developmental record deal with Warner Bros. in the late '80s, and things started to heat up around 1989 or 1990. I felt like I was jumping right into how it works, getting to write songs on Music Row with huge writers. My first write with Stewart Harris, we wrote "You and Forever and Me," which became a big hit for us a couple years later.

I knew we were a part of something different because of what we were, which was six young twentysomethings with hair down our back that looked like Poison, and [we] had no facial hair. Somebody said, "You're like surfers playing country music," and we knew something different was happening. We knew there was a wider appeal to this music, and the visual part is about to be something more than what it is has been in the past. It was the reason we happened, the reason we existed. It was long hair and southern rock.

Then Garth Brooks was smashing guitars—we knew we wanted to bring a rock-and-roll show to it. Being so young, we did it naturally as performers. We were a symptom of what was about to happen. We were the first generation to be influenced by more than just straight country. We were influenced by Van Halen. People would say we were a failed rock band, but that wasn't true. We loved country and got it, but we loved rock as well. It was destined to happen—people who had grown up on the Eagles were getting record deals. With that came an attitude of wanting to put on more of a show. We loved Aerosmith, Cheap Trick, Sammy Hagar, AC/DC and Ted Nugent—but also Emmylou Harris. Naturally, we were more into performing. We wanted to put on a show.

What was the atmosphere on Music Row in the '90s?

It was quaint and neighborhood-like, so casual and laid-back compared to L.A. and New York. You just found some old house and a place to park. You had no GPS or phone to find it, and it took about thirty minutes of looking. You found the house, had some coffee, wrote until noon, went to

Virginia's Market was a go-to lunch place for songwriters during the '90s. *Elizabeth Elkins.*

the Murder Mart [Virginia's Market] to eat lunch, saw four or five other couple/trios writers you knew. It's hard to describe, but very much just like meeting friends.

There was a sense in the '90s that country was printing money—that it was now equal to pop and rock. It felt more like just a boom. You watched Reba McEntire build Starstruck, and the labels all had seven imprints and forty or fifty acts. It was: This is the way it's going to be forever.

What was the best part of being a hit artist in the '90s?

The arena tours. I had Van Halen's guitar tech hand me a guitar, with nine more on a rack with a leather strap ready to go. It was the being completely taken care of—and have people go nuts every night. It was such a blast to be a part of that kind of top-scale touring experience.

What was the hardest part?

Being on the road and not having a life was the hardest part. By 1997, we had worked so hard to get there, following the music biz credo of "You better get it while you can." It took its toll. There were times you walked on the bus and you just can't stand anybody—too much pressure, too much partying, too much road. I don't think it's the norm for bands to tour as much as we did. At the peak, we played around 180 shows a year.

What were some of your favorite places on Music Row then?

So many are gone that I don't remember. The house that was Warner Bros. on Division was my favorite. We would go over there after hours on Sunday, we could use the phone to call home and charge it to the record label. Our career got started there at the catfish fry in that building. It was cool to see them move to the new building, I guess. We knew it was big business—but we miss the charm.

When did the boom stop and why?

Clear Channel bought all the radio stations. It affected us. We took 1996 off to recharge and not kill each other. When we came back in 1997, there were more suits, it was more corporate and Clear Channel was buying up stations. It already in one year felt so different. I remember thinking *Uh oh!* We would go visit radio stations that used to be independent, and suddenly it was a cubicle, one-room-next-to-every-other format. Country stations used to care. They cared if Alan Jackson was a star; they hooked their wagon to artists they loved. After Clear Channel, radio didn't care about creating and cultivating big stars. Now they don't support as many acts, and they all play the same thing.

Then, obviously, CDs went away. Digital came in. People listened to music differently. Everything changed.

What is the legacy of '90s country music?

We're still writing the answer to that question. It took it forever to go away, and when it did, we got bro-country. Now, people who loved it back then are getting empty-nested and asking what happened to country music. There seems to be a demand to go back to the roots of '90s stuff, and people want to hear it again. Hopefully it will always be a return point when things get too lost.

Garth Fundis

Producer (Trisha Yearwood, Keith Whitley, Don Williams)

What was the atmosphere on Music Row in the '90s?

Shania Twain joining with producer Mutt Lange really changed the direction of things. Everything was starting to sell multi-platinum. Everything was escalating as Soundscan came into play. Nashville offices had been branches of the big corporate labels, but Soundscan tied everything together. All of a sudden you have artists like Twain, Faith Hill and the Dixie Chicks start to ring the cash register, so the corporate bosses thought, *Holy shit, they are making money*. All of a sudden, they care what's going on in Nashville. In the '80s, Jimmy Bowen had already shifted the way we did business, and Lange bringing the rock-and-roll continued that. Loyalty started to become something that wasn't affordable. Everything was focused on the bottom line and what could propel the bottom line.

Describe your work as a producer in the '90s, and how has that changed today?

I just saw my first album with Trisha Yearwood [self-titled, released in 1991] was no. 8 on the best-selling albums of the decade, so I guess we did something right. When she and I met, I was enthralled with her. I knew I could help; I knew what to do. We put on a showcase at Douglas Corner, in the days that if you did a showcase at a club, people showed up. She knew a ton of songwriters, and she started passing out her cassettes to them, advertising herself as a demo singer to them. Eventually, everybody knew who she was. I booked it around [record label heads] Joe Galante's and Tony Brown's schedule. She packed the venue. Everybody knew she could sing and we had great songs, and they both loved it. People really showed up for things. Today, it's busier but not more relevant. It was easier to have relationships in those days.

Recording was just starting to move to digital at that point. There were generally a lot more studios on the Row than there are today. I had been working at Cowboy Jack's studio on Belmont Boulevard for many years, and I bought it in 1991. I owned it for twenty years and mostly worked out of there.

I don't think the boom of the '90s changed how I make records. I focus on the song first. But in those days, not as many artists wrote their own songs, so publishing companies had a much easier go of things. But for me, it's always been about casting the right characters in the studio. You have to mix the right players with the right song with the right artist, and that's still true today. I never made records because I thought they would sell—I made them because I wanted to make great records.

Did Music Row go global?

I think it did. The attention from New York and L.A.—and the actual sales numbers being available in real time from Soundscan—made it clear it went global. At that point, country was starting to crossover. People did become international stars. Don Williams and I had been working together since the '70s. He toured all across Europe for decades, and I was able to go on many of the trips. People really did pay attention; they knew details of country records that the average American listener did not know. They were ready for the numbers to explode.

When did the boom stop and why?

Did it stop? Napster had a big effect on all genres, though it took a while for country to catch up. The amount of CDs sold between 2000 and 2014 drops the numbers in half from the previous decade. It was slower here, but it happened. People moved online. Record companies had to trim their rosters and their employees. They had to be careful of their overhead, which didn't matter in the '90s.

What is the legacy of '90s country music?

It's a decade with a lot of really great music that comes from a lot of different influences. People who were having hits didn't know George Jones and Merle Haggard as much as they had a rock and pop background from the '70s and the '80s. The artists who came of age in the '90s were influenced by so many different kinds of artists. What came at you as a kid affects what you think is acceptable as country music. All of that goes into the evolution of how country music got to where it is today.

Chapter 13

You Don't Know What You've Got 'Til It's Gone

Lost Buildings of the Row

Elizabeth Elkins

My vision was a parking lot," Jerry Bradley jokingly told a crowd of music industry executives and stars in 2019 at the CabaRay Showroom, an establishment some fifteen minutes west of Music Row. He was telling the story of when his father, Harold, was buying up all the lots around the RCA Studios for $35,000 each in the 1950s. "I remember where Decca Records is was just a garden, but I figured we needed more parking lots," he laughed. The audience responded with several shouts of "It ended up that way!" and "You were right."

CabaRay owner Ray Stevens was quick to respond. "[Music Row] was a great place," he told the crowd. "Now it's more a campus for Vanderbilt and Belmont Universities. You're going to hit somebody riding a scooter if you go now. Maybe it's still a great place, but I'm glad I don't need to go there anymore." There were mixed cheers and subtle boos.

Stevens, once a critical part of Music Row's atmosphere, had just sold two of his properties there. One, a group of several early twentieth-century bungalows at 17th Avenue and Grand Avenue, sold for more than $11 million to a developer for a glass tower office building; and another, an acre lot at 1701 and 1707 Grand Avenue for $6 million, also went to a developer. The former was connected to a family trust with guitarist Chet Atkins.

His two massive sales were just two of many during a year when the National Trust for Historic Preservation put Music Row on its "11 Most Endangered Places" list. With more than sixty of five hundred of its potential

Historic Register–eligible properties demolished between 2013 and 2019, the Row is changing daily, with most older homes being replaced by condos and larger office towers. There is a heated debate about what should be saved, and how, and whether the fact that the music industry has simply outgrown these unique but limited spaces is at the heart of the problem.

Arguing aside, there is no doubt that these small houses and ramshackle studios made some of the greatest music of the twentieth century. Grammy-winning songs were written in attics and basements, and platinum-selling, life-changing albums were recorded up and down the alleys and side streets of the avenues. Those music makers fell in love and got wasted, broke up and got in fights, signed deals and found religion in the dive bars and restaurants along the way. Here is a look at just a very few of the now-gone spaces that made Music Row what it is.

Florence Crittenton Home for Unwed Mothers, 1815 Division Street

Lovingly referred to by many as "the Old Warner Building," the Crittenton building began as a home for unwed mothers in 1930, later becoming the home of Warner Bros. records through the 1980s and later a series of small offices and studios that included spaces for musicians such as Butch Walker and Brendan Benson of the Ranconteurs. Benson famously told co-writers as late as 2015 that his studio was plagued with ghosts to the point that the specters often disrupted recording sessions. The three-story mason building was known across the industry as a unique and special space.

"It was funky and had problems," explained publisher Matt Lindsey, who had an office on the third floor. "And it was definitely haunted. I remember being in there at night and hearing voices and walking out in the hallway and nobody was there. You had to have a key to get in, and nobody was there. I would go down the halls knocking on doors to see if somebody was there, but nobody ever was."

The building was loved despite the fact that owners tended to only half-fix the issues. The roof always leaked, and dead animals were often the cause of a terrible smell coming from the HVAC system.

The Crittenton building was torn down alongside the neighboring Spirit Music offices (808 19th Avenue South, circa 1974) between 2016 and 2018 to make way for Kenect Nashville, a luxury apartment complex.

The Crittendon Building was built for unwed mothers but later housed Warner Bros. records and numerous studios. *J. Totten Photo.*

A new development hides any trace of the Crittendon Building. *Elizabeth Elkins.*

TAVERN ON THE ROW / SAMMY B'S / FIGLIO'S ON THE ROW, 26 MUSIC SQUARE EAST

When it was built in 1906, this gorgeous blue brick/white trim house had no idea it would become a favorite watering hole on Music Row for many decades. Its early music industry use included offices for businesses such as *Billboard* magazine, Gold Standard Records, Brite-Star Promotions, Happy Wilson, Zeke Clements, Howard-Stone Publishing and Gra-Mar Talent Agency, which was co-operated by Barbara Martin, one of the first female executives in Nashville.

With a beautifully restored interior and intricate woodwork throughout, it housed multiple bars through the '70s, '80s and '90s, including BJ's Pour House, Toucan, Sammy B's and, finally, Figlio's on the Row.

But none was more infamous than the Tavern on the Row, known for the raucous cocaine-fueled parties that lasted into the early morning hours. People still joke that most people who hung out at Tavern on the Row can't remember anything about what happened inside.

"Everybody went there," explained Lindsey. "It was warm and inviting, and it was the kind of place you always wondered 'what the hell is going

Figlio's stood vacant for years before it was demolished in 2017. *J. Totten Photo.*

A vacant lot is all that's left of the famous "Tavern Full of Blow," also known as Figlio's and more. *Elizabeth Elkins.*

on.' [Songwriter] Harlan Howard was often there, as were all the stars and the legendary songwriters. I remember Tanya Tucker partying there all the time." Lindsey last visited the space when he signed songwriter Tony Arata (who wrote Garth Brooks's "The Dance") to a deal in 1994. "It was still in great shape then."

However, Warner Bros., which had purchased the building for nearly $2 million in 1989, eventually declared it structurally unstable, and it was torn down in 2017.

Looking for the "Tavern Full of Blow"? It's now a vacant lot.

Combine Music Publishing, 35–39 Music Square East

The home at 35 Music Square East, built in 1900, became the offices for Combine Music Publishing—a publishing company founded by Fred Foster of Monument Records. Songwriters on staff included Kris Kristofferson, Larry Gatlin, Bob DiPiero, Dennis Linde, John Scott Sherrill and Tony Joe White. Countless hit songs, including Johnny Lee's "Looking for Love," were written there.

Combine moved into the house in 1966 after a tragic event: the house's owner left one evening for a quick trip down to the corner store and returned to find his wife, Ima Jean, dead on the kitchen floor. He put the house up for sale soon thereafter. Combine turned the home into a series of offices and a basement studio known as the "Rat Hole." Songwriters wrote in the third floor attic space.

Woody Bomar, general manager of Combine, worked in the building from 1979 to 1987. He remembered it as a great space for songwriting and networking, for its incredible three to four day-long drunken Christmas parties and for its ghostly residents. "I heard plenty of ghost stories from the songwriters," he recalled. "They often felt they weren't alone up there."

Combine Music weathers the snow on 16th Avenue in 1984. The rear of RCA Studio A can be seen at back right. *Woody Bomar.*

In 1976, staff members held a weekend séance in the kitchen with a Ouija board to try to clear the air. They all got spooked when the figure of a woman was seen and called it off. Carolyn Sells—who worked at Combine as executive assistant to company head Bob Beckham for more than twenty years—knew that female presence very well. "There was a kitchen on the third floor," she recalled. "Songwriters said if they didn't keep it clean, Ima Jean would rattle the pots and pans to let them know she was unhappy."

Ima Jean, of course, was the wife found dead on the kitchen floor years earlier. "She always made her presence known," Sells continued, "and I would always talk to her, saying 'Goodnight, Ima Jean' when I left each evening."

Sells recalled a day she threw a piece of junk mail with Ima Jean's name on it into the trash. Immediately, electronics in the building stopped working: an electric pencil sharpener made strange noises and the studio went haywire. "Right then I got a call from the studio engineer in the basement," she said. "The recording board was doing wild things. So I talked to Ima Jean and explained it was junk mail and she knew it. A few minutes later, everything worked just fine again."

Writer/producer Alan Rush managed the studio. He described how the back entrance from the studio opened to the alley. "I would often hear somebody trying to open the door, but nobody was ever there," he said. "People often saw figures in the alley that never proved real."

Could it be possible that ghosts of one of the city's last public hangings were haunting the alley? In 1865, the city set up the gallows to hang a group of murdering thieves. The location matches up to the alley behind RCA Studio A and the former BMG Publishing and Combine locations. Or was Ima Jean the only ghost at work? Sells and Rush both remembered that she frightened one visiting band so much that the band refused to work in the studio anymore, completing their record elsewhere.

"Dennis Linde and I were in the basement producing," he said. "We didn't tell the band anything about the ghosts, and one guy went upstairs to use the bathroom. He came back downstairs, and he was white as a sheet, terrified. As he went up the stairs, he saw a lady's dress and old-time shoes as she went around the corner and closed the door to the bathroom. He waited for her to come out, but she never did. So he knocked, but the door was unlocked and nobody was there. Dennis and I looked at each other and said, 'Well, we have a ghost.' It took about thirty minutes to get everybody calmed down."

Generally, however, Ima Jean let the musicians and staff do their work. "Combine was such a creative hub for Music Row," Bomar recalled. "Lots

Former site of Combine Music at 35–39 Music Square East. *Elizabeth Elkins.*

of characters hung out in that house, the kind of folks we don't have on Music Row anymore. A lot of people hung out who weren't necessarily Combine employees or writers. They were friends of the family. Steve Earle would hang out there a lot. I remember it as a very creative place. It was a place you could just walk in and hang out if you knew somebody there, and you were always welcome."

The house was torn down in 2014 to build new offices for the Country Music Association and the publishing rights organization SESAC.

PILCHER-HAMILTON HOUSE, 1 MUSIC SQUARE WEST

Built in 1879, the Pilcher-Hamilton House was an incredibly beautiful red brick home that welcomed you to 17th Avenue, surrounded by tall oak trees and shade. Often described as "queenly," the house's surprise overnight demolition in 2014 was perhaps one of the most lamented architectural losses on Music Row. "People argued it was not historic, but it was so symbolic of

The Pilcher-Hamilton House in 1972. *Metro Nashville Archives.*

The site of the Pilcher-Hamilton House at the top of Music Row West, becoming a Virgin Hotel in 2019. *Elizabeth Elkins.*

entering the Row," said developer Steve Armistead. "I wanted so badly to save that building."

Armistead was one of many who tried. Publisher Pat Higdon recalled taking the elderly couple who lived there coffee and doughnuts every day for weeks, trying to convince them to sell him the house. But the couple's son had locked the property up in a trust.

Ironically, that couple's father had prevented significant Music Row development decades prior. In the early 1960s, the Music City Boulevard proposal would have changed the character of the neighborhood forever by significantly widening 16th Avenue to six lanes of traffic. Metro Councilperson James Hamilton lived in the home and objected to that plan. He formed a neighborhood group and successfully defeated it.

The Pilcher-Hamilton House—alongside 7, 9 and 11 Music Square West (each circa 1900)—was demolished to make way for a Virgin Hotel.

Mack's Café, 2007 Division Street

Opened in 1920, Mack's became so much more than a café as musicians flocked to the area. It was a perfect example of the numerous cafés around Music Row that are now extinct, including the Sunset Grill, J.J.'s Market and Noshville. With its "Business Is Great, People Are Terrific, Life Is Wonderful" sign behind the counter, Mack's was oblivious to the changing times.

In the '80s, it was open 24/7 and was a common stop for a hot meal after a write or recording session. Many bands, including Sawyer Brown, shot photos and videos and held album release parties there. Lindsey, who lived on Music Row at the time, recalled that he would often stop there for food after being out all night.

"I walked in around 2:00 a.m. and Johnny Cash and Waylon Jennings were sitting with Emmylou Harris in the corner," he said. "They were feeding the jukebox and the first song Emmylou played was John Anderson's 'Wild and Blue.' I guessed they were on a break from recording their Jesse James concept album."

Mack's Café was located where the Kimpton Aertson Hotel now stands.

New construction begins after razing several blocks around 19th Avenue and Broadway in 2019. J.J.'s Market and Noshville were both in the leveled blocks; Mack's Café was located near the center high-rise. *Elizabeth Elkins*.

PETE'S PLACE/PETE DRAKE'S RECORDING STUDIO, 815 18TH AVENUE SOUTH

Built in 1900, the nondescript house on 18th Avenue South was converted into a studio for session musician Pete Drake, who produced "The Stars of the *Grand Ole Opry*" series. It hit its stride when Mel Tillis bought it and used the studio for his publishing company. By 1986, emerging songwriters such as Buddy Cannon (who would go on to produce Kenny Chesney) were working around the clock in the space, churning out demos for new songs every hour. The studio hadn't changed since the 1970s and still had shag carpet and burlap on the walls.

It was torn down in 2013 to make way for the Artisan on 18th Apartments. Also on the chopping block for those apartments were three 1930s homes and the Fireside Recording Studios at 813 18th Avenue South, which was the early '70s recording home of Dolly Parton and Porter Wagoner.

145

CHAPTER 14

THE STORIES BEHIND GREAT SONGS

Brian J. Allison, Elizabeth Elkins and Vanessa Olivarez

JOE ALLISON

Jim Reeves' "He'll Have to Go"
Writers: Joe and Audrey Allison
No. 1 on *Billboard* U.S. Hot Country Singles, February 1960
Written at the writers' residence

Put your sweet lips a little closer to the phone,
Let's pretend that we're together all alone.
I'll tell the man to turn the jukebox way down low,
And you can tell your friend there with you,
He'll have to go.

How do you write a classic love song? "The answer is not very romantic, but I will tell you," remembered Allison about one of the classic hits of the early Nashville Sound.

The story behind the song is pragmatic in the extreme. Allison was working at Central Songs and had a long-running dispute with his first wife,

Audrey. She had a very soft voice, and whenever he called her at home, he couldn't understand what she said.

"Speak up," he said. "I can't. This is the best it's going to get," was the reply. Exasperated, Allison replied, "If you can't talk louder, put your mouth closer to the phone." This became a set routine between them, until one day when he came home to find she had written out the first line. They both liked it and got to work, knocking it out in no time.

They had intended to write a second verse, but when Freddie Hart wanted to cut it, Allison relented and decided it was as finished as it needed to be. Freddie never got to cut it, but a young singer named Billy Brown did and had a minor hit that came to the attention of Jim Reeves. Reeves fell in love with the song, and at the end of 1959, he cut it at RCA Studio B on 16th Avenue. In January 1960, it was released and quickly became Reeves's biggest hit, staying at no. 1 for fourteen weeks. It crossed over into the pop charts and was *Billboard*'s no. 2 song of the year—beaten out for the no. 1 spot by Percy Faith's "Theme from a Summer Place." It was nominated for two Grammy awards in 1961.

In the years to come, it would be recorded in fifteen different languages and by many other artists, such as Tom Jones, Eddy Arnold, Elvis Presley, the Mills Brothers, Roy Clark and Nat King Cole. It even went out of this world: in 1965, during the Gemini 7 endurance mission, astronauts Jim Lovell and Frank Borman sang the Cole version to each other to keep awake.

But Reeves's version, driven by his dramatic octave drop on the word *low*, would become the classic. Allison later remembered with a chuckle that most folks didn't remember the title. When people asked what he'd written and he told them "He'll Have to Go," they rarely seemed to recognize it. But if he sang the first couple of lines, they invariably said, "You wrote 'Put Your Sweet Lips'?"

And how would he classify the song itself? "It's a lost love song," he said in a later interview, "but it's a positive approach to the problem."

MARK NESLER

Darryl Worley's "I Miss My Friend"
Writers: Tony Martin, Mark Nesler, Tom Shapiro
No. 1 on *Billboard* U.S. Hot Country, September 2002
Written at 1109 17th Avenue South

I miss my friend
The one my heart and soul confided in
The one I felt the safest with
The one who knew just what to say to make me laugh again
And let the light back in
I miss my friend

Mark Nesler remembers very well the day in mid-summer 2001 when writer Tony Martin called him for some melody help on a song Martin and Tom Shapiro had started.

"I had been writing with Tony for many years, probably since 1995," Nesler said. "He told me they were stuck melodically. Tom asked him what he usually did when he got stuck on the music. Tom replied 'I call Mark Nesler.' They called me right then and there, and I'm glad I answered."

Nesler was invited in shortly thereafter to their writing room on the second floor of 1109 17th Avenue South, a building owned by Garth Brooks's manager, Bob Doyle. The yellow brick building, next door to the studio where Waylon Jennings was busted by the DEA for drugs, was an office space for many of the top (or soon to be top) songwriters in town: Jim Collins, Michael Dulaney and Rivers Rutherford all had rooms on the hall, while lawyers worked downstairs.

There, Martin explained that the title of the song "I Miss My Friend" came from the movie *The Shawshank Redemption*, where Morgan Freeman's character says the phrase exactly after his friend escapes from prison.

"They told me they didn't want the chorus to soar; they wanted it to be reflective," Nesler said. "I had the idea to start a chorus on the five chord [the fifth chord of a traditional musical key's chord option, generally reserved as a passing or resolution chord] rather than the usual one chord. This way, it would fall down into the one chord, rather than soar up to it. I brought that idea in with me, and they thought it was great."

"I Miss My Friend" was written at 1109 17th Avenue South. *Elizabeth Elkins.*

Nesler, however, didn't have a verse melody in mind, so he asked the other two for a week's time. "Songwriting gets so rushed today," Nesler explained. "That's nerve-wracking to me because you don't have time for songs to marinate. Songs will tell you when they are right. I wanted some time to get it right."

The verse melody Nesler brought back to 17th Avenue the next week stuck. The trio felt like they had a hit and immediately demoed the track. It was a session, Nesler recalled, where the band argued over the chorus chords because of his unorthodox musical setup.

Tim McGraw passed on the song before it hit the ears of Darryl Worley. Worley knew he had to record it. "I'd gotten to know this older lady who had a nine-year-old daughter. The relationship had progressed to where I thought I would introduce her to my family," Worley told *Country Music Notes*. "She and her daughter went away for a week, to Florida. The day before she was to come back home, I talked to her on the phone and told her I was going to take her to meet my mom. But they were killed in a car accident the next morning. There was no closure, no chance to say goodbye. She went away and left this feeling in my heart. It was horrible. [When I heard] 'I Miss

My Friend'—it was therapy; it was like a million pounds were being lifted from my shoulders."

"I remember the label was thrilled because the song started taking off on radio without any promotional money behind it," Martin said. "It immediately connected with listeners."

It was Worley's first no. 1, setting his career on fire. "I Miss My Friend" was a kickstart for the writing trio as well, who went on to write hits such as "You Look Good in My Shirt" for Keith Urban and "Living and Living Well" for George Strait.

BOBBY TOMBERLIN

Diamond Rio's "One More Day"
Writers: Steven Dale Jones, Bobby Tomberlin
No. 1 on *Billboard* U.S. Hot Country, March 2001
Written at 15 Music Square West

Last night I had a crazy dream
A wish was granted just for me
It could be for anything
I didn't ask for money
Or a mansion in Malibu
I simply wished for one more day with you

"It all started with just that first verse," Bobby Tomberlin explained, talking about one of the most powerful and popular country songs of the twenty-first century's first decade. "And it was a song that never would have happened if my co-writer's publishing house hadn't caught on fire."

Tomberlin was at home in his apartment on Old Hickory Boulevard when the idea first hit him. "I wasn't trying to write a song," he continued. "It was the holiday season, and I started thinking about people no longer in my life, some people I'd lost to death or relationships that went south. That verse just fell out. It was a gift from somewhere else. I recorded it quickly and very emotionally. I wish I still had the recording because I know I was crying."

Co-writer Steven Dale Jones was a staff writer for Island Bound Publishing, and just a week prior to their session, in late 1999, the Island Bound building

Number 15 Music Square West, where a piano in a room led to "One More Day" for Bobby Tomberlin and Steven Dale Jones. *Elizabeth Elkins.*

on 18th Avenue South caught on fire after an employee left a candle burning. Because of that, the two met up to write at 15 Music Square West, a then colorful, odd building that didn't even have a name. Island Bound had moved songwriter Roger Cook's piano into a room there while their building was being repaired. It was immediately clear there was some of Cook's "I'd Like to Teach the World to Sing" magic in those four walls.

Tomberlin shared the first verse that had hit him like lightning. "Stephen never played piano," Tomberlin explained. "But it was there, and he just had one little piece in the key of C—he said, 'Let me see if it fits what you've got.' Immediately it did." In fact, Jones's piano lick became the main melodic hook in the chorus.

The pair finished the song quickly and turned a rough recording of just piano, guitar and vocals in to their companies. It was pitched around and immediately held for Brooks & Dunn. It was Diamond Rio, however, that recorded it. The song continued to take twists and turns, as Dale Earnhardt died a few weeks after its release and a special version was recorded for him. The terrorist attacks of September 11 came soon after its chart run, sending

Left to right: Sara Evans, Eddy Arnold, Merle Kilgore and Bobby Tomberlin at the "One More Day" no. 1 party in 2002. The song has now surpassed 5 million radio plays. *Bobby Tomberlin.*

it back up the charts and into crossover territory as a Top Ten on the Adult Contemporary chart.

"We always say had there been no fire, this song would have never happened," Tomberlin added. But he's certainly glad it happened the way it did. "There's not a show I play that somebody doesn't come up to me afterwards and talk about somebody they lost and that song and how it helped them get through it," he said.

JIM MCCORMICK

Brantley Gilbert's "You Don't Know Her Like I Do"
Writers: Brantley Gilbert, Jim McCormick
No. 1 on *Billboard* U.S. Hot Country, July 2012
Written at Warner Chappell Music, 20 Music Square East

'Cause you don't know her like I do
You'll never understand
You don't know what we've been through
That girl's my best friend
And there's no way you're gonna help me
She's the only one who can
No, you don't know how much I've got to lose
You don't know her like I do

McCormick was writing at Warner Chappell, and by 2009, he and a young, unsigned Georgia artist named Brantley Gilbert had run into each other a few times in the hallways of the publishing giant's tan, stone building. McCormick recalled:

> *We were familiar with each other but hadn't written before that day. I'd even seen him play in some small Georgia clubs. He was on the phone with a buddy when I arrived—it was in one of those themed writing rooms they used to have, a beach theme or a barnyard theme, something silly. And this will teach you the value of listening to people more than your own self— because the answer is probably not inside of you, or you would have gotten it already. I just started listening because he was having a conversation about personal matters, but not so personal that he's not having them in front of me. After about fifteen minutes I realize the call is not going to end soon. He was saying some very pithy things.*

McCormick opened his laptop and started jotting down things Gilbert was saying. "He was on the phone maybe a half an hour. When he got off, he was super apologetic and regretted he used up so much time. I said, 'That's fine, because you said a few things that were real great.' I turned my laptop around and showed him."

Brantley Gilbert and Jim McCormick wrote "You Don't Know Her Like I Do" in the Warner Chappell Music offices at 20 Music Square East. *Elizabeth Elkins.*

Gilbert picked up a guitar immediately, and the two were off to the races on a gritty, vulnerable song that would later be released on the deluxe edition of Gilbert's *Halfway to Heaven* album. "I'm a real title guy, so I seized on that phrase immediately. We wrote it about as fast as I have ever written a song," McCormick continued. "It was full of the realness and the authenticity of his life that day. It's truly just a conversation he had with a friend saying—'Thank you, I got this.' That was the X factor in that song. We patted each other on the back and went on our way. It took maybe a couple hours."

Two years went by. When McCormick's deal was ending, he asked Warner's BJ Hill if he could demo the songs he'd written with unsigned artists who now had record deals. Hill obliged, and the song was recorded on a double session at producer Mickey Cones's place.

"The next thing I remember is running into Brantley's day-to-day manager at CMA Fest at Nissan Stadium in a VIP suite," McCormick said. "He told me he thought I had a cut on Brantley's debut record on Big Machine. Scott Borchetta had asked to hear everything Brantley had that wasn't on the initial independent release, which was being repackaged with bonus tracks. Mine was one of them."

In typical Nashville good luck fashion, the next update was that "You Don't Know Her Like I Do" was going to be a single. In July 2012, it became Gilbert's second no. 1—McCormick's first.

Matraca Berg

Deana Carter's "Strawberry Wine"
Writers: Matraca Berg, Gary Harrison
No. 1 on *Billboard* U.S. Hot Country, November 1996
Written in a house at the corner of Blair Boulevard and 25th Avenue

It was arguably the song that made every little girl in America long to be a country music singer. Recorded by sweet-voiced singer/songwriter Deana Carter, for her debut album *Did I Shave My Legs for This?*, it was released on Capitol in September 1996. The tear-jerking coming-of-age tale of innocence lost, "Strawberry Wine" was written by Berg and Gary Harrison at her home at the corner of Blair and 25th Avenues, just a block or two off Music Row official. Berg had just moved in with her now longtime partner, the Nitty Gritty Dirt Band's Jeff Hanna.

"Jeff had been living there alone for a while, and there was a spare room he used basically for storage," Berg explained. "One month, when he was on the road, I cleaned it all out and painted it dark blue. He had all kinds of cool old concert posters and gold records and awards. I had only a few—my Wall of Fame would come much later. So I hung up all his stuff and set out memorabilia on shelves. He had a black sofa and chair in the living room that I did not want as the first thing in the house you see when coming through the front entrance. I put those babies on a rug and dragged them down the hall to finish the writing room. It was awesome and moody and inspiring. That room would give me five no. 1 songs."

They say the best songs are written through experience and honesty—that can evoke the realest emotions simply by telling the truth as it was. This song was no different. Berg brought the title and general idea to Harrison, who sat eyes wide and scribbling away on a yellow legal pad, hanging on

Pat Higdon and Matraca Berg hold up their BMI Million-Air Awards at his office at 2004 Wedgewood Avenue. *Pat Higdon.*

Berg's every word so to not miss a beat. The two had worked together many times and had developed a style to hone their creative process.

"He is a master of simple, yet powerful imagery," she explained. "The two of us together just click. I'm more flowery, and he's down to the bones. That is why it works. We thought it would maybe be an album cut someday. It was so different and specific in story."

Little did they know how big the song would be. It all began when promising young Carter showed up to a small showcase and hotdog grill-out that publisher Pat Higdon threw for labels, producers and artists to come and hear the new songs within his writers' catalogue.

"Deana was the only artist to show up," Berg recalled. "She loved the song. We didn't really think of it as something potentially life changing for her. We were all completely caught off guard when she released it as a first single."

"Strawberry Wine" debuted on the charts in August 1996 at no. 70 and, to the surprise of the team, crawled its way to the top in November, holding the top chart position for two weeks. The song was also the Country Music Association's Song of the Year and is still beloved by country music artists and fans alike.

MARK IRWIN

Tim McGraw's "Highway Don't Care"
(featuring Taylor Swift and Keith Urban)
Writers: Mark Irwin, Josh Kear, Brad Warren, Brett Warren
No. 4 on *Billboard* U.S Hot Country, May 2013
Written at Big Yellow Dog Music, 1313 16th Avenue South

It was the third single off Tim McGraw's 2013 album *Two Lanes of Freedom*, and it featured two of the hottest artists in the genre: Taylor Swift and Keith Urban. Written by Mark Irwin, Josh Kear and Brad and Brett Warren (known famously around Nashville as the Warren Brothers), the song was penned at Big Yellow Dog Music at 1313 16th Avenue South.

"Josh had a comfortable studio space on the top floor of Big Yellow Dog," Irwin explained. "We would always write on Mondays, but this particular day, Brad and Brett joined us. We started around 11:00 a.m. and wrote until late afternoon. Josh was sitting behind his keyboard next to his computer. The Warrens and I were spread out with our guitars on two couches. We knew that McGraw needed some songs, so we were focused on writing a hit for him."

The song came together rather effortlessly—on a lucky day, it happens that way. "Josh had the title and a rough concept in his head," Irwin continued. "I remember Brad sitting down at Josh's keyboard. He started playing, and that created the vibe that turned into the song. Then, like always, we all tossed out lyrics and maybe melody ideas until the pieces all fell into place."

Typically, a song would go directly to the publisher to critique. Then, a current-sounding demo is recorded to "pitch" the tune to various artists who fit the vibe and theme of the track. From there, with a lot of luck and perfect timing, the song will hopefully be "cut" by an artist who connects with it. This instance was different. At the time, Irwin was writing for McGraw's producer, Byron Gallimore, who was all set to produce the accomplished superstar's next masterstroke. What's more is that the Warren Brothers already had a previous professional relationship and a great rapport with McGraw. Needless to say, the writers didn't have any real trouble getting it into the hands of the people who mattered. McGraw heard it and loved it.

During the recording of the album, it was McGraw's idea to feature a female vocalist on the song and move the single into the "event" category (for awards shows). There was talk of McGraw's wife, Faith Hill, singing with him. However, Swift proved to be the perfect pairing, and the rest is history. "Highway Don't Care" was a hit and earned the team numerous awards.

"I'm just surprised it worked out at all," Irwin laughed. "So often things like this don't pan out for whatever reason—scheduling, label problems, loss of interest—but for this tune, the stars aligned perfectly. Thank God!"

Chapter 15

Three Chords and the Truth

Secrets of Success

Vanessa Olivarez

Every day, hundreds of aspiring artists and songwriters move to Nashville. They arrive with stars in their eyes—they cannot wait for their turn through the "Nashville machine." That machine is a complex set of parts and gears that turn sometimes when you least expect it but often after years of hard work. There are artist managers, record producers, record labels, publicity teams, radio promotion teams and publishers, all of whom must work together in concert to create an "overnight success." Some say that luck and that age-old theory of "right place, right time" still holds its own—even through the broken-ladder state of the current music business, where the climb seems more arduous than ever. There are still those glimmers of hope that shine through like a warm light and remind you that anything and everything is still possible in Music City.

Behind every successful artist is a team. An artist spends years assembling the perfect one, waiting for that right time where the pieces come together and the stars align to create country music magic. It usually starts with a publisher or a manager who works tirelessly to find a record label for the artist. Then a record label brings in a radio team, booking agency and publicity team to spread the gospel. However, everybody has a different path, and most often, those pieces don't fall together perfectly. Instead, it's often all chaos before it works. But in every case, it takes a team.

THE PUBLISHER: DANIEL LEE, ALTADENA MUSIC

Daniel Lee is a song man. As a publisher for Altadena Music, he was a key ingredient in the success of both songwriter Hilary Lindsay and Big Machine recording artist Carly Pearce. The role of a publisher is, in short, to find the best songs in each writer/artist's catalogue to either "demo" (a track made as an example of what the fully produced work could sound like) to pitch to other artists to record or to decide which ones to keep to help an artist on their team navigate their own path to ultimate success. Every day, these artists and writers go into stark office spaces across Music Row—fingers crossed—in the hopes of writing a hit song. A song that will finally take on a life of its own and land them in the place they felt they always belonged. After the writing of the song is complete, a "worktape" (an acoustic one-take recording typically captured on a phone or similar recording device) is submitted to the publisher for review. Then the future of the song is decided—whether it will need to be edited, demoed for pitch opportunities, kept for the writer/artist to cut themselves or thrown into the dirt pile with the other hundreds of thousands of songs that never see the light of day.

An early job at Island Bound Music gave Lee the experience he would need for a lifetime of successful song plugging. "I learned so much from the writers there," he said, "about how things have worked in the past, about how things were changing and how to hopefully connect the dots moving forward. My bosses there and subsequent jobs gave me enough rope to just figure it out on my own. That's where I really started to develop some of my specific ways of doing things that I still carry with me today."

Those learned tricks of the trade became the steppingstones that led to the immense amount of success he would see soon after. While at Ten Ten Music Group, Lee landed his first big placement: Reba McEntire's "Turn On the Radio." It went no. 1.

Eventually, Lee left Ten Ten and accepted the position of senior creative director at BMG Music Publishing. There he began to pitch songs by Hillary Lindsey, a multi-hit songwriter. Her brilliant compositions were not easy to sort through, according to Lee, as the majority of them came to him already almost perfectly crafted. They made a winning team.

It was at BMG that he also took aspiring young artist Carly Pearce under his wing. It was not an easy climb for Pearce, but with Lee's unwavering belief in her talent and fervor and cutting-edge pop/country producer Mike Busbee (Maren Morris, Keith Urban, Kelly Clarkson, Florida Georgia Line,

Daniel Lee, general manager and VP of creative for Altadena Music. *Daniel Lee*.

Timbaland) at their side, she soon became a raging success with her first no. 1 song, "Every Little Thing." Lee remembered the hardships and obstacles Carly had to face on her way up the mountain.

"As somebody who really had been kicked in the teeth and who a lot of people had written off, she just didn't give up," he explained. "She has something to say, she has a vision, she knows who she is and she's just extremely talented. A lot of her triumph was frankly just trial and error. It was her getting into writer rooms and me trying to beg people to write with her—and just stumbling closer to something that felt like something and sharing the music to figure out what feels like it could be that 'thing.' Carly stands out for me as one of my favorite success stories because of everything it set in motion."

However, the journey wasn't without its curve balls and surprises. "I think we all thought that first song was a really great song for her without question, but it wasn't the song that we were planning to lead with. It was actually a Hillary song that she cut—it was an outside song. Then Sirius radio started playing it, and it all just blew up from there. She thought that was going to derail all of these plans that we had. What I told her was, 'Let's make the best of a good situation.' There's nothing wrong; there's nothing bad with this exposure. Best case scenario is this song blows up, and if it doesn't, it's just going to create a nice up ramp to whatever we were going to come in with first anyway, and then it wound up at no. 1."

Sometimes on Music Row, a bit of rob-your-neighbor ends up coming into play, albeit unintentionally. On the tails of her first hit single, her next song, "Hide the Wine," originally cut by Little Big Town, headed up the charts to no. 13.

"I remember the first time I played Carly that song, Little Big Town had actually already recorded it," Lee recalled. "The day we found out it wasn't making their album, I booked studio time and we got in and recorded it because we knew that that was the song."

Lee also worked extremely closely with producer Busbee. While working at BMG, he connected Busbee to up-and-coming songwriter/artist Maren Morris. The two immediately hit it off in the writing room and began their work together on Morris's first major label album, 2016's *Hero*. Busbee and Lee soon realized that they had a knack for working together and were a natural and effortless team. Soon Lee decided to take a leap of faith into a new business venture in partnership with Busbee, called Altadena. He recounted how this alchemical combination came to be—and wildly serendipitously.

"I think the idea of us doing something together was something that we had both been aware of for a while," Lee said. "It just happened that his new publishing venture when he left BMG, created the opportunity for Altadena to become a reality. Then the other partnerships with Warner records and Red Light came together with some preexisting relationships that he had. Then my contract with BMG was coming up at the end of the year, and they very graciously allowed me to go and pursue this opportunity. Sometimes it happens that way, and sometimes when it does it's like a sign from the universe."

He unabashedly cited Busbee as his biggest mentor and source of encouragement, and it appears that many people in country music and otherwise would say the same thing of the highly creative genius. Sadly, he passed away from brain cancer in 2019, leaving behind a body of work with Gwen Stefani, Keith Urban, Pink, Katy Perry, Florida Georgia Line and Garth Brooks.

Sometimes, all it takes to succeed is the undying faith of someone you admire. Much in the way Busbee inspired and supported Lee to follow his bliss, Lee has helped to elevate the careers of dozens of songwriters and artists hoping for their shot through the combination of belief, talent and a seasoned ear.

THE RADIO PROMOTER: ED GREEN

Another step in the ever-winding staircase to musical success is the ever-challenging, always present, widespread speaker that is the radio. Ed Green is a radio promotion expert. He has worked at high levels of radio promotion in New York and Los Angeles for numerous major record labels and eventually for Dave Matthews's Red Light Management, which led him to Nashville.

Green is perhaps most famous for breaking Nirvana into the mainstream with its second album, *Nevermind*:

> *When* Nevermind *came out, I was the Philly/Baltimore/Washington guy for David Geffen Records, and Nirvana was playing a place in Philly called JC Dobbs. It holds 350 people tops. The stage might be like ten by twelve, and there were hundreds of people outside. The show was incredible, people were freaking out, the video was all over MTV. Basically, the album exploded. After the show, we booked this tiny dressing room, and we tell the band that the record's already gold after the first day, and they had 400,000 more orders on the album. 400,000 more! Krist Novoselic* [Nirvana's bass player] *was like, "Wait, What? W—what are you talking about?! The record on day one is already certified gold, and it's going to be number one?" We even had Top 40 guys play it who said they would never play it. That day was the coolest.*

The job of a radio promoter is certainly a challenging one. It takes persistence, dedication, passion and a heavy dose of influence. In a nutshell, after the recording of a song is complete, the song is sent to Green or someone similar, who will then take that song to different program directors and try to "turn them onto" the singles they want that station to "add" (which is another way to say put the song on rotation). Then they must formulate a plan to convince the stations to play the song in heavier rotation so the song can gain familiarity and popularity. However, as everyone has learned at one point or another in their lives, asking for something is never easy. The art of swaying someone is fine-tuned only after years of practice.

"Radio promotion is super hard," Green explained. "You basically start at no 95 percent of the time. It's very rare when you take a brand-new artist and get them airplay. Anybody can get Luke Bryan played now, but they just don't play a lot of new product. It's basically starting at no and delivering information to convince the radio programmers that they need to play this record and why. They may like it, but to get them to actually commit to actually playing it in a real, regular rotation, you have to have a really great relationship with the people who run the station—and you have to be able to deliver information and show them why. The stations know their audience. That's what they get paid to do. We get paid to break artists, so we have to give them information on both sides to convince them that this will work for them. It is their job on the line if they get bad ratings. But if you're passionate about the song, you need to have them put ears on it and have them give the record a shot."

In addition to Nirvana, Green played a major part in the radio success of Guns N' Roses, Lady Antebellum (now Lady A), Maren Morris, Kristian Bush, Sam Hunt, Cher, Counting Crows, Don Henley and the Highwomen. When he moved to Nashville, he was struck at the difference between pop and rock radio and country:

> *It's so different. It's like night and day. The country music side is much more of a tighter community. When you are working rock and pop records, a lot of those records cross formats. Country records and programmers are a much tighter community. There's more big events to attend, showcases to go to, and radio programmers like to come in and see artists play. In my opinion, better relationships are built. Country artists do pretty much everything for radio, and radio has a great relationship with the country artists. In other formats, there's not that marriage. On the whole, country artists and the radio guys are really good partners together. We'll have Dierks Bentley go and do Bobby Bones and drive himself there. If you asked a pop artist—any pop artist—to drive themselves to a radio station for an interview…well, you'd probably get monkeys flying out of your ass before you would get that to happen! But Dierks will get in his truck and drive and get there. Same thing with Maren or Sam Hunt, Chris Stapleton. Any of these artists that I get the pleasure to work with. They work their asses off. I feel like the country radio community is much more of a community.*

While the sense of community and friendship that passes between the country artist and associated program directors can be reassuring, there is a downside. Because country radio is so finite, and there are so many musicians vying for their spot in the countdown, a record can carry with it the burden of time. As Tom Petty said, the waiting is the hardest part. "It takes forever to work a record up the country chart because there is so much product and it's only one format," Green continued. "You can work a record for forty to fifty weeks. Easy."

A radio promoter is often involved from the first time they hear the demo. Green noted that Lady Antebellum's 2019 record came out in November, but he probably had the demos for eight months before that. The artists will then finish the master recording of the songs in between tour dates, and then those masters are sent to the label, but not without a great deal of preparation. Green said that he'll work with the label and radio as much as six months in advance of a record release.

Although radio is losing popularity in other formats, Green believes that it's here to stay in country:

> *The current structure of country radio is huge. It's huge because that's how music is mainly getting consumed. People aren't buying. There hasn't been any artist that has broken without having a song on the radio. Not one. It is and will always be king. In an iHeart radio presentation, they presented us with the data that 93 percent of listeners say that they still discover music from listening to it on the radio more than any other means. I still think radio is the primary driver to reach the biggest mass audience. People are punching buttons in their car radio no matter where they are going.*

In order to succeed these days and really push a single to its peak performance level, Green noted that artists have to have a "get your hands dirty" work ethic. Constant fan engagement and an iron-clad social media presence can make or break a performer's singles, concert and the longevity of their career.

In the end, though, as Green noted, you've got to have a great song. Still, part of the fate of a song's lifeline is reliant on that magic unknown ingredient that makes it a hit. The kind that crashes into you like a wall of feeling that you can't stop. After years of listening to hundreds of hit songs, Green has developed quite the ear for the songs that will succeed.

"I've learned how to recognize that in artists such as Sam Hunt, Brett Young and Maren Morris," he explained. "You could just sense something when you'd see them play for the first time. When you hear a song sometimes, the hair on your arms starts standing up and you're like, 'Holy shit! That's the one!' Those kinds of moments don't happen often. A hit song is a rarity."

Obviously, everybody's ears are different on Music Row. While a publisher might think one song is the obvious hit, the artist's manager might think another is the obvious choice and the artist yet another. It's all a grand guessing game. Everyone is placing their bets on opinions—praying that the opinions of the masses will align with the choice they made.

"Well, when I hear a song—and it doesn't happen often, but I get this feeling. I knew it with 'Smells Like Teen Spirit' [Nirvana], 'Can't Get You Outta My Head' [Kylie Minogue], 'Livin' La Vida Loca' [Ricky Martin] and Sam Hunt's 'Take Your Time.' I worked all of these songs. You hear that kind of song and it's a one-listen thing—and you can't wait to call radio and tell them you've got one."

The role of a radio promoter within the artist's career is a valuable one that is so often overlooked, but without radio folks like Green to push them through the seemingly steel ceiling of country radio, an artist may be stuck—no matter how talented they are. It takes a leader and a diligent personality, belief in the product and a never-quit kind of drive to help find the spotlight at the end of the tunnel. That's how an emerging artist can find their way out of music purgatory and into the small society of artists who can say they've had a no. 1 song.

The New Artist:
Lainey Wilson, Broken Bow Records

At the time of this publication, Lainey Wilson is just at the beginning of her record label journey. When we spoke, she was on the road on her first radio tour, visiting radio stations and working with people similar to Green to share her songs to a wider country music audience.

As a child in Louisiana, she knew she wanted to pursue the Nashville dream. After years of singing and playing in school and her local area, Wilson finally decided to take the leap of faith, pack her things and head to Music City. She switched to online classes to finish college, and she lived in an extended-stay hotel for a while. Although she started meeting some other songwriters, the fact that she was under twenty-one and couldn't go to bars and writers' nights made it hard to network. Her parents bought her a camper to live in, which she was able to put on land belonging to her mentor, songwriter Jerry Cupit. They wrote together every day. When he passed away, she had to sell the camper and find an apartment. Finally old enough, she spent any free time attending writers' rounds and concerts to make new connections. She met songwriter Forrest Whitehead, who helped

Lainey Wilson onstage at CMA Fest, 2019. *Cece Dawson.*

to point her in the right direction, connecting her with performing rights organization ASCAP's new artist program.

In Nashville, it's often about random connections. At her new apartment complex, she met Mandelyn Monchick, a budding music manager who had recently moved to town to manage Sony artist Kasey Tyndall. "We all became friends, and her and Kasey would write," Monchick explained. "One day, when Kasey was out of town, Wilson came over and played me a song that her and another co-writer had written. It was so good that I had to do something. I started sending songs out but I don't think I ever got a response."

But that didn't stop the promising entrepreneur. Monchick continued to set up co-writes and small showcases for Wilson. A co-write at Sony turned into a publishing deal when a creative staff member there heard her other songs.

"This is about showing up and being there. Lainey lives for the 'no pain, no gain' philosophy. She can look at things objectively and doesn't easily get her feelings hurt. She's somebody who treats people well. I never have to sell her to somebody," Monchick explained. "If they don't like it, I have nothing else to say. I just have to be able to share the facts, and the music needs to sell itself. I think somebody's music has to start catching on after a year or couple years on its own. If that doesn't happen, then maybe you need to move on. At the end of the day, it is a business. We haven't struck gold every single time with Lainey, but there definitely has not been a time where we've questioned our partnership or the direction we are going."

Soon, Wilson signed a record deal with Jason Aldean's label, Broken Bow Records. Knowing who you are without a doubt as a performer is by far one of the most important pieces of the puzzle. The team's vision of Wilson's trajectory was clear-cut. The two knew what they were after and were certain that the sound they wanted could best be created by hit record producer, Jay Joyce. Through a series of connections, they were able to reach Joyce as well. He was equally sold on Wilson's hard work ethic and talent. They recorded an EP together, and the label sent Wilson out on her radio tour.

The future of her career is unknown. It's an aggressive sort of waiting game that both frustrates and excites simultaneously. "The careers that I would like to shadow a little bit are people like Reba," Wilson said. "You gotta be hard working and not willing to quit. If this is your livelihood, then you have no other option. You have no choice but to make it work. So you kind of have to have that mentality that there is no Plan B. It's important to stay true to yourself because people can read through anything. It's about authenticity."

Much of an artist's sound lies in the hands of a skilled producer. In the same way that Jay Joyce molded Wilson's reverie into something tangible, performers everywhere are looking for their perfect partner to help shape theirs. A producer is more than just pushing buttons and turning knobs on a board. A producer is a musical visionary—someone who can take the songs and ideas of a singer-songwriter and paint them into a work of art—a finished product for all ears to enjoy. Each sound—down to the type of guitar, the amplifier used on that guitar and the emotion within the vocal performance—is decided by the producer. Think of them as a map—someone to help navigate the ever-changing, always confusing path to the silver-lined cloud that is fame.

THE PRODUCER: DANIEL TASHIAN

Daniel Tashian is a highly coveted producer, songwriter and artist. As the son of Barry and Holly Tashian, a country/folk duo, Tashian grew up with music constantly in his ear:

> There was a point as a kid where I just became obsessed with music. It was after my freshman year. I got out of the party pot-smoking scene and into the singer songwriter mode. I was really blown away by some of the '90s folk singers like Suzanne Vega and Shawn Colvin, who could create a whole autobiographical world with just a guitar and a voice. Then I got a four-track cassette for my fifteenth birthday and I was hooked. That was it. I just loved to overdub my voice and hear the chords and the blend. I also really loved U2 quite a bit and thought I wanted to be a frontman in a band for a second—but that seemed like a lot. I couldn't really find musicians to play like I wanted them to without being told anything until my band Silver Seas started in '99.

Tashian also connected with fellow Nashville songwriters to form the band Skyline Motel and has an ongoing (and recently Grammy-nominated) children's music project.

Many believe that people who are artists themselves become better and more creative producers. Tashian, realizing his love for production equaled his love for writing and performance, initially began making records for others "out of necessity." His new venture started when a new artist called A Girl Called Eddy e-mailed and asked if he would help her—although the album took ten years to finish.

"I guess it happened because I wasn't really able to make much of an impact as an artist—even though I did some good things," Tashian explained. "I always loved music and being in the studio and playing, so producing records was the next logical choice. It's been really eye-opening to see how ideas can really travel so much farther with a great artist when they have a great team around them. I'm just really lucky it worked out because if it didn't, I don't know what I would have done. I can still have my own artist life, but producing gave me a career. Do I still have aspirations as an artist? Of course. I'm curious, and I like to explore what kind of moods and sounds I have within myself. It's a lifelong journey that you never leave."

As a staff songwriter for Big Yellow Dog Publishing, his songwriting credits show just how creative he can be—with songs by artists ranging from Kacey Musgraves's "Slow Burn" to Little Big Town's "Nightfall" to Leon Bridges's "God Loves Everyone." Influenced heavily by the melodic intervals in electronic music, Tashian's unique savant-like genius for lyric makes him a goal producer for many performing artists. When asked about his writing process, he answered that most times, it's about tapping into his subconscious:

> There's a deep pool of music I've heard—and love that I've felt in my heart. I try to close my eyes and get into that water. When I'm co-writing, I try to find something going on inside the artist—where their energy and inspiration is leading them and go that way. There's a sort of interview process where I ask questions like "Where are you from?" "What were you like as a kid?" Then I like to use paper and pen—not the computer. And some songs come out better than others. Who knows why? You enter some situations with the best intentions and it turns out okay. Other times, you get no sleep and have no ideas and it ends up being amazing. I can't explain it.

He stated that the qualities he watches for when considering joining forces with another artist starts with an undeniable voice, a willingness to collaborate and a spirit of good intention—as well as "a kind of grit where they can bounce back from all the setbacks and still bring joy to the table. I think it's also timing and a personality that can handle what comes, along with a certain kind of chill. Also some good people around them who encourage and bring out the best. A kickass team around them never hurts either. That way, people will hear the stuff you do."

Tashian's lush production work caught the attention of Kacey Musgraves. The two originally met casually around town, but when Tashian's friend (and bandmate in Skyline Motel) Ian Fitchuk suggested she come over to co-write with them, they had no idea that their trajectory would change forever. Bringing in a loop he had created on his iPad, they wrote their first song together, "Oh, What a World." Around the same time, Sheryl Crow offered Tashian the use of her studio while she was on tour. Armed with the feeling that he, Fitchuk and Musgraves had something magical, he invited the two of them to join. It was there that they began to construct the bones of what would soon evolve into Musgraves's 2019 Grammy-winning Album of the Year, *The Golden Hour*.

As a Nashville native, Tashian has witnessed the constant change in both the business and architectural side of Music Row. Still, one thing hasn't shifted much: the need for a robust dose of "try"—the tenacity of someone born for the limelight.

"Making it in Nashville is about time and experience. Maybe you sort of do your time over there and get rejected a lot and you develop a thick skin and get used to disappointment. Maybe that's the role Music Row plays. I never know what to think when someone moves to Nashville and has immediate success," he said. "I think I'm somewhat stubborn and a slow learner. I wrote my ass off for eight years before I really got anything going. It is quite an experience to get a bunch of people weighing in and telling you that you didn't make the grade over and over—'cause that's what it is. And then when something works, you sort of feel astonished. But I wouldn't trade that for anything. It made me who I am, and I enjoyed a lot of the process, the journey."

"Making it takes love," he concluded. "Putting the extra time and attention in—because I love doing it so much. That's what works"

THE BIG SUCCESS: KRISTIAN BUSH OF SUGARLAND

Kristian Bush has been down Wilson's path, has worked with hit producers like Tashian, spent countless hours on the road with relentless radio promoters like Green and had his songs worked by publishers like Lee—all as a part of the multi-platinum selling duo Sugarland. As of 2019, he is now forging a solo career after a long-term, extraordinarily successful run with radio and sales success. This East Tennessee–born singer-songwriter and multi-instrumentalist has always had the music inside him. As a child in the early 1970s, Bush convinced his parents to let him move from violin to guitar, and he hasn't looked back since.

Kristian Bush of Sugarland
in 2019. *Kristian Bush.*

By age fourteen, he and his brother, Brandon (now an accomplished keyboard player who has played for Train, Black Crowes and others), were sending tapes of songs they had written off to record labels. "I was rejected about once a week," Bush laughed. "It was my first taste of 'no.'"

He did find a label home in time with a duo called Billy Pilgrim, which signed to Atlantic Records on the strength of his incredible songwriting. This led to more and more writing connections. That band found moderate success but never took flight. A chance connection with Atlanta songwriter Kristen Hall led to a brainstorm idea: he would join the new country project she was brainstorming. The pair wrote numerous songs together and auditioned various female lead singers (author's note: I was one of those singers and wrote several songs with Bush and Hall for the project) before settling on Jennifer Nettles, who had already established a huge regional career based on her own songs and powerful voice.

"By the time Jennifer arrived into the band," he explained, "Kristian and I had dozens of competed songs for her to learn. She came in and sang songs that were already written, and you know this because you wrote some of them with us. The idea was to write all the music and then see what we could do with it. It was a deeply ambitious project from the beginning. We wanted to be in a tour bus, not a van. Which when you start a band, is almost an impossible idea."

Ostensibly overnight, the band was asked to showcase at Nashville's 12th and Porter bar. The crew drove the four hours from Atlanta up to Music City and, unbelievably, signed a record deal that day. Bush claimed that the light-speed success of the band was a combination of feeling "provider anxiety" with the arrival of his first child and the magic of knowing finally that it "wasn't just about him":

Things get much easier when it's not about you. I tell people this all the time when they are trying to have a solo career: the moment it's not about just you, you are able to support it and champion it like never before. It's not wrapped up in your ego. People will believe in a thing much faster than they will believe in a person. I think that was also a cool thing about Sugarland. It had an interesting identity. You could squint your eyes just right and understand it wasn't about any one person, even though it was totally about Jennifer's voice singing that stuff. Everybody knew she was awesome but just hadn't dug into the right songs or dug into the right platform. It did go quick, but from the outside. From the inside, it went a little bit slower because we immediately get signed, but we went to the label and sat on our hands for a year and a half.

When the label finally released the single "Baby Girl," it sky-rocketed up the charts to no. 2. But the band wanted more. "It was pretty freaky because we had gone through an entire album that was pretty successful. It sold tons of copies but had no no. 1 songs on it. So for us, we had this reality check. You can make it without a no. 1. Everyone thinks that they are going for this incredible touchdown, but you can win a game with a whole different set of ways to score points."

While making the second album, the band lost Hall, who left the band due to stress. With the band now a duo, they realized that they would need to refine and alter their writing process a bit. Bush decided it was time to "go fishing."

"I had a box that I've carried with me my whole life, a cardboard box full of sheets of lyrics that are partially done. They are just songs I started and didn't finish—or words that I liked that I had to depend on my memory to remember the melody," he explained. "If I didn't, I would just have to use the words and work them in a new way. It wasn't really organized. It was literally a cardboard box full of crap, some of them were napkins or receipts, all random pieces of paper. We reached into that box several times during that second record. We just pulled the ideas out and wrote songs off of them."

Bush credits that, and the introduction of new co-writes, as key to developing the identity of Sugarland. The change of approach paid off in 2008 when their second album, *Enjoy the Ride*, produced two no. 1 songs. By their fourth album, Sugarland had sold more than 14 million albums. As of 2019, Bush continues to write and play with Sugarland and his new project, Dark Water. He's also moved more into a producer role, most successfully with Canadian artist Lindsey Ell and country crooner Frankie Ballard.

"I'm more of an 'artist whisperer' than a producer," he joked. "Labels often want me to get the artist's head straight rather than to produce. But in time, the artist will always lead the way. I often ask artists what they were listening to the last time they really enjoyed listening to music, and I send them off by themselves to do some work. And that work is for them to record a homemade cover version of the album that made them feel that way."

That work usually is on a 1990s-style four-track recorder, with just a guitar, a shaker and a microphone—a work intended for nobody but Bush. That's how Ell's version of John Mayer's *Continuum* was born. But in time, Ell's team was so impressed by the artist's rendition that they decided to release it to the public.

Similar creativity help light Ballard's career on fire. Ballard said he felt underused as an artist. Bush asked why. "Frankie says, 'I have seen every Elvis video ever. I've imitated and memorized all of his moves,'" Bush recalled. "Then he showed me a whole bunch of his moves—in my living room. I thought, holy shit, he's one of the few people on Earth I know who can actually pull that off because he's handsome—and there is also a preacher somewhere in him. So, I suggested that for the next song we write that we don't write a single line without having a matching move that goes with it." The resulting song was "Try Try Try."

So what is Bush's secret to success? "A thick skin, a willingness to forgive yourself, a tough work ethic and a supportive team that allows the artist to simply be the artist," he said. "Different people put us on this expectation wheel. Once you start putting yourself on top of other people's expectation wheel, you just live constantly disappointing other people or yourself. Living like that starts to break your heart at a higher rate. An artist is a very resilient human, but if you break their heart faster than they can repair it, they stop trying." He concluded:

Also, work your ass off. Just do the work. Everyone wants everything to be naturally easy, and it was never easy. It was never easy to call somebody and book a show. It was never easy going to rent a van. The dream is big, and if you've got the dream, then the other pieces that go with it are just the work you put into reaching that dream. Now, if you've misnamed your dream or you've absorbed someone else's dream or you saw a dream on TV and you think maybe you want that dream, or even if somebody next to you has a dream and it's intoxicating to be next to them, well then it's different. You're gonna give up quicker. But when that dream is yours, it gets even more dangerous. And if you can get two or three people walking in the same direction with a shared dream, even if it's just a Venn diagram of where they cross, you and a manager, you and a singing partner, you and a band, you and a producer…if you can figure out where those things meet, that shit is dangerous. If you're good at dreaming, then fuck. You better strap yourself in. You're gonna make it happen or it's going to happen to you when you're busy sleeping.

BIBLIOGRAPHY

Chapter 1

Adams, George Rollie, and Ralph Jerry Christian. *Nashville: A Pictorial History*. Norfolk, VA: Donning Company, 1988.

Burt, Jesse C. *Nashville: Its Life and Times*. Nashville: Tennessee Book Company, 1959.

Davis, Louise. "DeMonbreun Burial Spot Still a Mystery." *Tennessean*, January 5, 1986.

————. "Mysterious DeMonbreun Comes into Clear Focus." *Tennessean*, May 19, 1985.

Demonbreun, David Henry, and James Edward Demonbreun. *Family Ledger*. Nashville: Tennessee State Library and Archives, 1860–1902.

Drolet, Yves. *Dictionnaire Généalogique et Héraldique de la Noblesse Canadienne Française du XVII au XIX Siecle*. Montreal: Dico, 2010.

Phillips, Betsy. "In Search of Granny 'Rat's Tavern.'" *Nashville Scene*, October 27, 2009.

————. "Where's Elizabeth Durard's Statue?" *Nashville Scene*, August 17, 2009.

Provine, William. *Jacques Timothe Voucher: Genealogical and Biographical Data* folder. Nashville: Tennessee State Library and Archives.

————. Joseph Deraque Folder. Tennessee State Library and Archives, Nashville, Tennessee.

Simons, Bunny. "Timothy Demonbreun—The Noble Frontiersman." Timothy Demonbreun—The History and Legacy. http://www.timothydemonbreun.com/Timothys_Story.html.

Summerville, James. *Southern Epic: Nashville through Two Hundred Years*. Glouster Point, VA: Hallmark Publishing, 1996.

Tennessean. "Two Centuries of Nashville." April 28, 1909.

Walker, Hugh. *Tennessee Tales*. Nashville, TN: Aurora Publishers, 1970.

Whitefort, Kathryn de Monbreun. *A Genealogy and History of Jacques Timothe Boucher Sieur De Monbreun and His Ancestors and Descendants*. Ann Arbor, MI: Edwards Brothers, 1939.

Wills, Ridley. *Nashville Streets and Their Stories*. Franklin, TN: Plumbline Media, 2012.

Zepp, George R. *Hidden History of Nashville*. Charleston, SC: The History Press, 2009.

Zibart, Carl F. *Yesterday's Nashville*. Miami, FL: E.A. Seemann Publishing, 1976.

Chapter 2

Clements, Paul. *Chronicles of the Cumberland Settlements, 1779–1796*. N.p.: self-published, 2012.

Cox, Isaac Joslin, and Reginald C. McGrane, eds. *Quarterly Publication of the Historical and Philosophical Society of Ohio* 8, no. 2 (1913).

Scott, Sir Walter. *Rokeby: A Poem*. Edinburgh: John Ballentyne & Company, 1813.

Smith, C. Alphonso. *Selected Stories from O. Henry*. New York: Doubleday, 1922.

Smith, Reid. *Majestic Middle Tennessee*. Gretna, LA: Pelican Publishing Company, 1982.

Chapter 3

Collins, William. "Tennessee Spirits—Ghosts of the Volunteer State." Haunt Jaunts. www.hauntjaunts.net/tennessee-spirits-the-ghosts-of-the-volunteer-state.

Pursell, Julie. "'Haunted House' to Be Auctioned." *Nashville Banner*, December 4, 1974.

Traylor, Ken. *Nashville Ghosts and Legends*. Charleston, SC: The History Press, 2007.

Zepp, George R. *Hidden History of Nashville*. Charleston, SC: The History Press, 2009.

Chapter 4

Armistead, Steve. Interview with Elizabeth Elkins, Nashville, July 25, 2019.

Associated Press. "Evangelist Tony Alamo's Followers Sell Suspect Goods as He Awaits Sex Abuse Trial." July 13, 2009.

Belmont Church. "Our History." https://www.belmont.org/who-we-are/our-history.

Brackett, Carolyn, and Robbie Jones. United States Department of the Interior, National Register of Historic Places Multiple Property Documentation Form, September 30, 2016.

Cumberland Presbyterian. February 7, 1901, 177.

Douglas, Mason. *Now You Know Nashville.* Nashville, TN: Wild Cataclysm Press, 2016.

Fields, Pat Bolton. "Don't Mention Stone Walls, Miller Horn Has Had Enough." *Nashville Tennessean Magazine* (November 16, 1952).

Flynn, Katherine. "Nashville's Music Row Is Waiting for You." National Trust for Historic Preservation blog, November 28, 2017.

Hall, Douglas. "Residence for Aged to Close." *Tennessean*, October 21, 1969.

Morley, Steve. "The Crossroads of Contemporary Christian Music." *Sports and Entertainment Nashville*, May 7, 2014.

National Register of Historic Places Inventory Nomination Form. "Little Sisters of the Poor Home for the Aged." June 26, 1985.

Nelson, Carrington. "Former Home for the Aged Finds a Fountain of Youth." *Tennessean*, May 17, 1999.

Nesbit, James N. *A Lifestyle of Light.* Lancassas, TN: Robert Hugley, 1996.

Oermann, Robert K. "LifeNotes: Evangelist, Costumer, Record Maker Tony Alamo Dies." *Music Row Magazine* (May 5, 2017).

Phillips, Betsy. Interview with Elizabeth Elkins, Nashville, July 26, 2019.

Tennessean. "Elderly Sisters Die Only a Half Hour Apart." December 3, 1955.

———. "Little Sisters of the Poor First Began Their Noble Work in France." September 3, 1916.

———. "Prayer of the Little Sisters." December 31, 1909.

Williams, William. "Property for Sale at Key Music Row Intersection." *Nashville Post*, June 21, 2018.

Zepp, George R. *Hidden History of Nashville.* Charleston, SC: The History Press, 2009.

Chapter 5

Allison, Joe. Unpublished manuscript, 2002. Author's possession.

Kingsbury, Paul, ed. *The Encyclopedia of Country Music*. New York: Oxford University Press, 1998.

Kosser, Michael. *How Nashville Became Music City, U.S.A.: 50 Years of Music Row*. Milwaukee, WI: Hal Leonard Corporation, 2006.

Nelson, Willie, and David Ritz. *It's a Long Story: My Life*. New York: Little, Brown, & Company, 2015.

Sutherland, Frank. "9 New Buildings Slated in Music Row Plans." *Tennessean*, October 16, 1968.

Thomas, Susan. "Country Music Neighbors Call the Row Home." *Tennessean*, October 7, 1979.

Whitt, Wayne. "Boulevard Bust: Wrong Way on 1-Way Street?" *Tennessean*, December 20, 1970.

Chapter 6

Brackett, Carolyn, and Robbie Jones. United States Department of the Interior, National Register of Historic Places Multiple Property Documentation Form, September 30, 2016.

Bryant, Dane. Interview with Carolyn Brackett, Nashville, June 27, 2015.

Ghianni, Tim. "The Legends Who Made Endangered Music Row Are Gone." *Tennessee Ledger*, June 14, 2019.

Gray, Michael. "Made in Nashville: 50 Great Albums that Showcase Music City's Diversity." June 20, 2003. CMT.com.

Mendelson, John. *Harvest* review. *Rolling Stone* (March 30, 1972).

Nashville Banner. "Wesley Rose Says 'Pop City' Outlook Hurts Music Row." August 1977.

Oermann, Robert K. "Nashville Remembers Leonard Cohen." *Music Row Magazine* (November 14, 2016).

Ronk, Liz, and Lily Rothman. "See Historic Photos of Bob Dylan and Johnny Cash in Nashville." *TIME* (March 26, 2015).

Sanders, Daryl. "Looking Back on Bob Dylan's Blonde on Blonde, the Record that Changed Nashville." *Nashville Scene*, May 5, 2011.

Simons, David. "Recording *Harvest*: The Making of Neil Young's Classic 1972 Album." *Acoustic Guitar Magazine* (July 2001): 34–41.

———. "Tips from the Top: The Making of Neil Young's 'Harvest.'" *BMI Songwriter 101* (June 11, 2007).

Sisk, Chas. "Curious Nashville: The Year Jimi Hendrix Jammed on Jefferson Street." *Nashville Public Radio Podcast*, December 15, 2016.

Wilkins, Jason Moon. "How Time in a Tiny Cabin Near Nashville Revived Leonard Cohen's Songwriting Career." *Nashville Public Radio Podcast*, March 3, 2017.

Chapter 7

Allison, Rita. Personal interview with Brian Allison, Nashville, 2019.

Billboard 85, no. 8. "Tape Presence, Bomb Threat Cause House Clearing at Opry" (February 24, 1973): 28.

Dickerson, Diane. Personal interview with Brian Allison, Nashville, 2019.

Ferguson, Carrie. "Nude Songwriter Turns Heads on Music Row." *Tennessean*, February 15, 1996.

Oermann, Robert K. "Country Queen Faces Career Crossroads." *Tennessean*, August 6, 1987.

Chapter 8

Adams, Henry. "The Sources of Country Music." Nashville, TN: Country Music Foundation, 1989. https://countrymusichalloffame.org/content/uploads/2019/04/Thomas-Hart-Benton.pdf.

Callison, John. Phone interview with Brian Allison, Nashville, 2019.

NEA. "Thomas Hart Benton's Final Gift." https://www.arts.gov/about/40th-anniversary-highlights/thomas-hart-bentons-final-gift.

PBS. "About Thomas Hart Benton." https://www.pbs.org/kenburns/thomas-hart-benton/about-benton.

Chapter 9

Castino, Alex. *American Revolutions: Wanted! The Outlaws*. Nashville, TN: CMT, 2005–6. Television special, accessible via YouTube.

Gantry, Chris. Interview with Vanessa Olivarez, Nashville, November 4, 2019.

My Heroes Have Always Been Cowboys. Directed by Leo Eaton. Alpine, TX: Independent, 1983. Documentary, accessible via YouTube.

Chapter 10

Brinton, Larry. "Girl, 11, Beaten, Ravished." *Nashville Banner*, July 16, 1965.
———. "Police Find No Clues in Bludgeon Slaying." *Nashville Banner*, October 16, 1964.
Dau's Blue Book of Selected Names of Nashville and Suburbs. New York: Dau Publishing Company, 1907.
Horstman, Dorothy. *Sing Your Heart Out, Country Boy*. New York: E.P. Dutton & Company, 1975.
Sutherland, Frank. "Rapist Draws 120-Year Term." *Tennessean*, March 16, 1967.
Tennessean. "Hopkinsville Quizzes Wilson." August 12, 1966.

Chapter 11

Appel, Kara, and Marion Kirkpatrick. "Music Row Staple Bobby's Idle Hour Closes." January 4, 2019. WSMV.com.
Browning, Graeme. "Maude's Courtyard: Spirit of Gentility." *Tennessean*, May 18, 1978.
Gallagher, Kathleen. "Radio Exec 'Repents.' 'Eyesore' Bar Memorial Held." *Tennessean*, December 23, 1978.
Gibson, Frank. "…And Then They Lower the Boom." *Tennessean*, March 22, 1974.
Glaser, Dennis. *Music City's Defining Decade: Stories, Stars, Songwriters and Scoundrels of the 1970s*. Bloomington, IN: Xlibris, 2011.
Howard, Melanie. "Harlan Howard Birthday Bash." Harland Howard website. https://www.harlanhoward.com/post/harlan-howard-birthday-bash.
Krantz, Sarah. "Maude's Courtyard Plans to Reopen in 1–2 Months." *Tennessean*, May 15, 1986.
Moore, Linda A. "Maude's Closing Down, Future Cloudy." *Tennessean*, July 2, 1992.
Sanders, Forrest. "Final Minutes at Bobby's Idle Hour Bring Music, Tears and Hope the Story Will Continue." January 14, 2019. WSMV.com.

Sawyer, Bobbie Jean. "The Boar's Nest: A Casual and Exclusive Hangout Where Stars Crafted Their Best Songs." Wide Open Country. wideopencountry.com.

Zeimer, Joe. *Mickey Newberry: Crystal & Stone*. Bloomington, IN: AuthorHouse, 2015.

Chapter 12

Bruce, Trey. Interview with Elizabeth Elkins, Nashville, September 26, 2019.

Fundis, Garth. Interview with Elizabeth Elkins, Nashville, October 22, 2019.

Higdon, Pat. Interview with Elizabeth Elkins, Nashville, October 17, 2019.

Howell, Porter. Interview with Elizabeth Elkins, Nashville, October 21, 2019.

Lewis, Pam. Interview with Elizabeth Elkins, Nashville, October 16, 2019.

Martin, Tony. Interview with Elizabeth Elkins, Nashville, July 25, 2019.

Mitchell, Sean. "Living It Up in the Grand New Nashville: Once Considered the Eccentric, Colorful Country Cousin of the Music Industry, the Home of the Grand Ole Opry Has Finally Made It Big." *Los Angeles Times*, November 7, 1993.

Nesler, Mark. Interview with Elizabeth Elkins, Nashville, July 25, 2019.

Chapter 13

Armistead, Steve. Interview with Elizabeth Elkins, Nashville, November 1, 2019.

Bomar, Woody. Interview with Elizabeth Elkins, Nashville, November 18, 2019.

Brackett, Carolyn, and Robbie Jones. United States Department of the Interior, National Register of Historic Places Multiple Property Documentation Form, September 30, 2016.

Bradley, Jerry. Comments at the Country Music Hall of Fame Artist Luncheon and Inductees Panel at Caba-Ray, Nashville, September 16, 2019.

Higdon, Pat. Interview with Elizabeth Elkins, Nashville, October 17, 2019.

Lindsey, Matt. Interview with Elizabeth Elkins, Nashville, October 31, 2019.

Rush, Alan. Interview with Elizabeth Elkins, Nashville, December 2, 2019.

Sells, Carolyn. Interview with Elizabeth Elkins, Nashville, November 25, 2019.

Stevens, Ray. Comments at the Country Music Hall of Fame Artist Luncheon and Inductees Panel at Caba-Ray, Nashville, September 16, 2019.

Williams, William. "Entertainer Sells Music Row Sites for $6M." *Nashville Post*, August 21, 2019.

———. "Historic Music Row Building to Be Demolished." *Nashville Post*, October 27, 2017.

Chapter 14

Berg, Matraca. Interview with Vanessa Olivarez, Nashville, October 28, 2019.

Billboard. "Brantley Gilbert Chart History (Hot Country Songs)." Billboard.com.

———. "Darryl Worley Chart History (Hot Country Songs)." Billboard.com.

———. "Diamond Rio Chart History (Hot Country Songs)." Billboard.com.

———. "Hot Country Songs: Strawberry Wine." Billboard.com.

———. "Tim McGraw Chart History." Billboard.com.

Henry, Shannon. "The Story Behind Darryl Worley's 'I Miss My Friend.'" *Country Music Notes*, July 30, 2011.

Horstman, Dorothy. *Sing Your Heart Out, Country Boy*. New York: E.P. Dutton & Company, 1975.

Irwin, Mark. Interview with Vanessa Olivarez, Nashville, October 17, 2019.

Martin, Tony. Interview with Elizabeth Elkins, Nashville, July 25, 2019.

McCormick, Jim. Interview with Elizabeth Elkins, Nashville, May 23, 2019.

Nesler, Mark. Interview with Elizabeth Elkins, Nashville, July 25, 2019.

Tomberlin, Bobby. Interview with Elizabeth Elkins, Nashville, June 26, 2019.

Chapter 15

Bush, Kristian. Interview with Vanessa Olivarez, Nashville, October 30, 2019.

Green, Ed. Interview with Vanessa Olivarez, Nashville, October 17, 2019.

Lee, Daniel. Interview with Vanessa Olivarez, Nashville, October 16, 2019.

Monchick, Mandelyn. Interview with Vanessa Olivarez, Nashville, October 20, 2019.

Tashian, Daniel. Interview with Vanessa Olivarez, Nashville, October 27, 2019.

Wilson, Lainey. Interview with Vanessa Olivarez, Nashville, October 20, 2019.

About the Authors

Elizabeth Elkins is a professional songwriter and writer. A military brat, she holds degrees from the University of Georgia and Emory University. She has written for the *Atlanta Journal-Constitution*, *Creative Loafing, Art & Antiques* and many others. She is president of Historic Nashville Inc. and the author of the upcoming *Your Cheatin' Heart: Timothy Demonbreun and the Politics of Love and Power in Nascent Nashville* (Vanderbilt University Press).

Vanessa Olivarez is a professional songwriter and vocalist. A Texas native, she was a Top 12 finalist on the second season of *American Idol* and received a Dora Award nomination for her work in the Toronto, Canada production of *Hairspray*.

Together, Elkins and Olivarez are Granville Automatic, an alt-country band that has been featured in the *New York Times*, *USA Today* and the *Bitter Southerner*. Their songs have been used in numerous television programs and films, and they have written songs recorded by more than seventy-five other artists, including Billy Currington, Wanda Jackson and Sugarland.

They were the songwriters in residence at the Florida-based Seaside Institute's Escape to Create program, where they wrote a Civil War concept album, *An Army without Music*. Their 2018 album, *Radio Hymns*, focuses on the lost history of Nashville, and the 2020 follow-up, *Tiny Televisions*, was inspired by Music Row stories in this book. You may have seen their videos on CMT. The pair live in Nashville, Tennessee, and regularly tour across the United States.

While not a musician himself, BRIAN ALLISON was born and raised on stories of country music. His father, Joe, was a producer, songwriter, radio personality and pioneer, and without his stories, this book would not have been possible. A professional historian, museum consultant and writer, he is the author of two other books for The History Press, *Murder & Mayhem in Nashville* and *Notorious Nashville*. He lives in Nashville.

Scan the QR code above or visit www.granvilleautomatic.com/book for links to stream or buy Granville Automatic's EP *Tiny Televisions* (six songs inspired by the stories in this book) and the band's album *Radio Hymns*, their 2018 record about Nashville's lost history.

Visit us at
www.historypress.com
....